GREAT JEWS I HAVE KNOWN

GREAT JEWS
I HAVE KNOWN

A Gallery of Portraits

By

MAX RAISIN

Biography Index Reprint Series

BOOKS FOR LIBRARIES PRESS

FREEPORT, NEW YORK

STANDARD BOOK NUMBER:

8369-8023-9

LIBRARY OF CONGRESS CATALOG CARD NUMBER:

71-117331

PRINTED IN THE UNITED STATES OF AMERICA

To My Grandchildren
KENNETH AND JOAN ROSENTHAL
AND
HARRY AND MICHAEL GRABOW

PREFACE

The essays contained in this volume first appeared in the *National Jewish Monthly* of the Independent Order B'nai B'rith for whose permission to have them reprinted I herewith express my sincere thanks. I also wish to state my deeply-felt appreciation to the many readers of the *Monthly* who wrote to me as well as to the editor of the magazine (where not a few of them were published) telling of their great interest in the essays and of their desire to see them appear in book form. It is indeed due to their encouragement that this volume is now made available to the reading public.*

My personal belief—which I state here at the risk of being deemed immodest—is that these twenty articles will be helpful in furthering an understanding of the period in which we are living. Despite the author's self-imposed limitation to avoid an exhaustive biographical portrayal of his heroes but to give only portrait sketches and close-ups of these eminent personalities whom he knew well, the thing to bear in mind is that these men and women were the products of a great age, an age which they themselves have helped to make great.

And this age is worth studying, for beyond the shadow of a doubt we are privileged to live in the greatest epoch in Jewish history since the destruction of the Jewish Commonwealth by the Romans and the beginning of the Dispersion, nearly 1900 years ago. We are eye-witnesses to the miracle of a resurgent Jewish nation in ancient Palestine, of an Israel come to life again after a suspended national existence of so many centuries. The sight of the return to the old homeland of the sons and daughters of a people so widely scattered over the face of the globe, has fascinated and thrilled the

---

*A Yiddish version of these essays also appeared in the Yiddish Monthly, the "Zukunft" and was published in book form by the Central Yiddish Culture Organization, New York.

entire world. And among those who have made this miracle possible are the men and women whom I have portrayed in these essays. It was Carlyle who said that the history of the world is the history of its great men. It is a truism which applies with special force to the history of the Jews during the period in question, i.e. the last 60 to 75 years.

To be sure, not all of the personalities I am here portraying consciously and avowedly worked for the consummation of this age-old dream of Jewish statehood. Indeed some, like Isaac Mayer Wise, were strongly opposed to it, for it belied their interpretation of Jewish history, which was in terms of religion only. And even those among them who supported the nationalist viewpoint not all were active in bringing it to reality. The important thing to remember, however, is that what they all had in common was their love and devotion to the Jewish people which each of them served in his own way, and whose survival they all wanted. Howsoever rabidly anti-Zionist men like Isaac Mayer Wise and Gotthard Deutsch may have been, by their insistence on a continued community life for the Jewish people, be it only as a religious group, they to that extent contributed to the survival of their people, the people out of which was to arise the national entity known as "Israel". Reform Judaism, at first so extremely opposed to Jewish nationalism, was destined to play its own important part in making the Zionist ideal possible, for the reason that no religious-minded Jew— and Reform Jews definitely are that—could long remain indifferent to what has been fundamental in Jewish thinking for nearly two millennia, the return of the Jews to Zion.

In the struggle between the two schools of thought, the nationalists won out against the purely religious view-point because they were on sounder historical ground. Their stand was more in keeping with the basic teaching that we are at one and the same time a people and a church, a people devoted to certain religious ideals but a people all the same, a people that began its existence as a sovereign nation and at the same time cherished the ideal of being or becoming a "Kingdom of Priests". The accident of the Dispersion in no way vitiated that ideal, but only made it a more vivid aspiration for millions of Jews, a lodestar on their weary road through dark centuries of homelessness and oppression.

Nor did the rise of the new era of emancipation solve the "Jewish Problem" for the majority of our people who remained in lands of political oppression. Even in democratic countries, political freedom failed to lessen social and economic discrimination, and often even acted as a spur for anti-Jewish sentiment on the part of governments and masses alike. The antisemite saw in the Jews not a religious but a racial entity, though the religious tag made racial recognition easier for him. It did not really matter to him what the Jew believed or failed to believe, a fact well expressed long ago by Germans: *"Der Juden Glaube ist einerlei; in der Rasse steckt die Schweinerei"* (What the Jews believe is immaterial; it is their race which is swinish).

Among the Jews themselves the religious urge, strong though it was, actually was subordinate to the group consciousness. Judaism as a religion more often than not was a divisive rather than a unifying factor. There were always dissident factions that warred upon each other, the Pharisees and the Sadducees in ancient times, the Karaites and the Talmudists in the Middle Ages, the Hassidim and Mithnaggedim of a century or two ago, and the Orthodox, Conservative and Reform elements of more recent years. All of them, however, felt united as a people, their religious zeal only lending greater emphasis to their unity. The one exception to this rule were the so-called assimilationists, who denied their affiliation with a Jewish people and, in consequence, became lost to Jewry religiously as well through the process of intermarriage and submersion in the non-Jewish majority.

One important fact brought out by these portrait sketches was the part played in the revived national life of Israel by East European Jewry, since nearly all of the subjects dealt with came from either Russia or Poland, Lithuania, Galicia, Roumania or Hungary. Even native Americans like Henrietta Szold and Judah L. Magnes, owed their interest in Zionism, to which they rendered such outstanding services, to the influence wielded upon them by their people's traditions, which were so zealously maintained in their homes, or to their contact with the East European Jewish masses. Zionism would not have won its astounding triumphs had it not been for the great reservoir of Jews in the Eastern European countries from which came the recruits and the leaders of the movement. It was these masses that made possible the career of Theodore Herzl who, but for their numbers, would have remained a general without an army. Israel's first President, Dr. Chaim Weizmann, is himself, of course, a product of the staunch idealism and loyalty which lived in those Jewish masses.

The story of a people's self-determination has never been more clearly illustrated than in this dramatic tale of millions of human beings taking their destiny in their own hands and bringing about their "auto-emancipation" (as Dr. Leo Pinsker expressed it) in the face of tremendous odds and difficulties that seemed insurmountable. The mere circumstance that it was a problem of self-redemption for eight to ten million people scattered in many lands and suffering direst economic poverty as well as political oppression and persecution, was what made it seem so baffling. By comparison, the task of Moses was simple and easy, since aside from the fact that there were but 600,000 of them, the people he took out of bondage all came from one country, Egypt, and all marched as a unit towards the Land of Promise. The Zionists had no such advantages; indeed, when Herzl first appeared upon the scene with his "Jewish State" there was not even a place to point to as a land of promise. Palestine was in the hands of the Turks.

Historians are sure to dwell upon this remarkable achievement, so singular in the annals of the nations. They will look for the sources of inspiration that gave the millions of Eastern Europe's persecuted and poverty stricken Jewish masses their faith and their courage, and they will find it in the very circumstance of their life as an oppressed and hounded minority.

Tragic as was the life of the six million Jews in the domain of the Czar, it yet had its many compensations. On the one hand the Russian Jews had no rights worth mentioning. They were confined to a "Pale" or settlement on the German and Austrian borders which exposed them to immediate danger in case of war, were restricted in their movements, excluded from educational institutions, limited numerically in the professions, and subjected to all sorts of indignities and frequent bloody assaults at the hands of the mobs. On the other hand they enjoyed a large measure of freedom in their religious and cultural life. The small towns of the "Pale" became citadels of spiritual living for those Jews; there life centered around the synagogue, which served as a rostrum for political discussion no less than as a "House of Study", in addition to being an outlet for the social life of the people. Under the cover of religious preaching, *Maggidim* (wandering Yiddish preachers) often expressed opinions surprisingly bold for a police state, and carried on the forbidden Zionist propaganda under the noses of the authorities to whom Yiddish was a foreign and unintelligible tongue. There was, of course, the ever present hazard of being caught, of informers working against their own people for whatever reward they might get for it; but the Jews were willing to take the risk, and often when in difficulties resorted to the tried old device of "Chabar" (bribery).

Life in those small Russian-Polish towns—which was duplicated to no small extent also in the Jewish communities of Austrian-held Galicia and Prussian-occupied Pozen—often presented an idyllic picture of a people ordering its spiritual life to suit its own needs and cravings and deriving great comfort out of it. The Sabbath was strictly observed, as were all other major and minor Jewish holidays. And there was a network of educational institutions beginning with the *Cheder* (elementary private school), taking in the *Talmud Torah,* a sort of public school which, however, was attended chiefly by the children of the very poor, and concluding with the *Yeshivah,* which was devoted wholly to higher Talmudic studies and from which came forth the rabbis of the communities, though many, perhaps most, of the students chose other vocations. But in the *Yeshivah* they satisfied their thirst for Jewish learning, and it was as Talmudically learned laymen that they took their places in the communities. This resulted in a laity which was Jewishly informed and inspired. Ahad Haam, Simon Bernfeld, Nahum Sokolow, Jacob Klatzkin, Bialik, Masliansky, were direct products of this educational system, and so were Shmaryahu Levin, M. M. Ussishkin, A. J. Stybel, and even Vladimir Jabotinsky and Saul Tchernichovsky, though the two latter received their Hebraic training somewhat indirectly. The potent influence exerted by the vast reservoir of the ghetto Jewries overtook them, too, as it did untold other thousands howsoever different the surroundings in which they found themselves.

In the United States there is now going on a controversy beween those who favor and those who oppose a system of "day school" education for the Jewish child, a kind of "Parochial School" moulded after the Catholic school system. In the Eastern European communities the Jews demonstrated the value of such a system. Out of it came the leaders, the fighters and the martyrs for the Jewish cause. The uprising in the Warsaw Ghetto, where the Jews knew they were trapped and doomed yet tenaciously struggled against overwhelmingly superior and well-armed forces, was made possible because of this spirit inherited from the *Cheder* and the *Yeshivah.* And so, too were the fighters in the Arab-Jewish war in Palestine. From President Chaim Weizmann and Prime Minister David Ben Gurion down the entire line, the men and women of the State of Israel have demonstrated the full importance and usefulness of a training which helps rear the "complete Jew". The State of Israel is a monument to such an educational system.

Involved herein is the question of the position of the Jew in America, which some claim is sure to be affected by the new Jewish State. Will antisemitism in the United States raise its ugly head even more menacingly because of this State? Should the Jew here lie low and suppress all interest in what is going on in that tiny nation on the shores of the Mediterranean for fear that it might adversely affect him in this land of freedom? To me all this seems but idle speculation. Nothing will stop the sworn foes of the Jew from venting their spleen on our people, whatever the provocation or lack of it. And by the same token, no amount of Judophobia in America will ever influence American Jews to lose their interest in Israel, or to stop aiding it in every proper way.

The forces that make history can not be affected by the likes or dislikes of individuals or of key groups. Today we are face to face with an established fact, Israel, which nothing can change or erase. The men and women I have depicted in my essays were both causes and products of these historic forces. They played the part imposed upon them, and their names will forever remain enshrined in the grateful memory of the people whom they have done so much to bring to life again as a nation.

Max Raisin

Paterson, New Jersey

Table of Contents

GREAT JEWS I HAVE KNOWN

Ahad Haam

A MAN OF SMALL STATURE, with a large bald head which seemed disproportionate to the size of his body, and eyes that peered at you through a pince-nez proudly but not unkindly—this was Ahad Haam when I first met him in the summer of 1909. That was a memorable summer for me. I had just been married and took my New York bride to Europe, planning to visit many of the old world's capitals and, wherever possible, look up some of the Jewish notables. We began our "grand tour" in London and with Ahad Haam. Meeting him was to me the fulfillment of a long-cherished hope.

It meant coming in personal touch with the man whom I had so greatly admired, and with whom I had corresponded for more than a decade, ever since he commissioned me to write a series of articles for his noted Hebrew monthly magazine, "Haschiloah". I was a mere youngster at the time, not more than seventeen, when this honor and responsibility fell to me. Ahad Haam, then living in Odessa, was at the acme of his literary career as a thinker and stylist. His collected Hebrew essays, published under the title of "Al Parashat D'rakhim" (At the Cross Roads), was a beacon-light and path-finder for the *Maskilim*, the Hebrew "enlightened" intellectuals of Russia and Poland, and cast a fascinating glamor upon all Hebraists scattered over the globe, including the United States. As an editor Ahad Haam was gracious and kindly, though not uncritical. My Hebrew was far from perfect, but he took pains with it and at the same time refrained from seeming the dictator. He corrected only where absolutely necessary, and in his letters kept encouraging me to send in more contributions.

I did not know then, what I discovered later, that his considerate treatment of me, as of others, was dictated as much by necessity as by a native gentlemanliness and refinement. Assuming the editorship of the first serious monthly ever to be published in Hebrew, Ahad Haam soon discovered that it was a most difficult task for the simple reason that there was a woeful lack of suitable writers. He had to develop his writers as well as manage his publication, and wherever he found a young man who, he believed, possessed a spark of talent, he did his best to bring the budding writer into his literary household. My first essay evidently proved acceptable to him for its contents, if not for its form, and he published it with some modifications, and then asked for more. Looking back at it now, half a century later, I realize that my relationship with this man was a determining influence during the formative years of my life. Physically I lived in New York, Cincinnati, or Meridian, Mississippi, but spiritually I found myself at the feet of this master in Odessa or in London, whither he had moved after the Czarist-inspired pogroms of 1905.

Here a word of explanation may be necessary. I am aware that I am writing for an American public at the end of the first half of the 20th century about men and events in 1898 and 1909. Some of my readers may not know that Ahad Haam was a pseudonym, but one which dominated the Hebrew literary world of those days to such an extent that it became permanently fixed in the public's mind so that the true name was all but forgotten. Few are the eminent writers in the world's literature of whom this could be said. Mark Twain was better known than Samuel Clemens, and Sherlock Holmes than Arthur Conan Doyle. In the neo-Hebrew world this was the only case of a man obtaining such prominence and popularity that he came to be exclusively known by his pen name. Other Hebrew writers attempted to hide their identity, but even so leading a writer as Mendele Mokher S'forim was also well known as Sholem Yakov Abramowitch. Ahad Haam's real name, Asher Ginzberg, was known to but very few readers of his books and essays.

Yet strangely enough, this man, who for decades reigned supreme over the literary world of his people, became a writer only by the sheerest of accidents. Until 1889, when he was already 33, he had never suspected that he was capable of writing, inasmuch as he had never attempted to publish anything. That year, at the urging of Alexander Zederbaum, editor of the Hebrew daily, *Hamelitz*, of St. Petersburg, he appeared in print for the first time with his article *"Lo Zeh Ha-Derekh"* (literally: This is Not the Way) which contained a vehement attack on the old *"Hibbat Tzion"* (Love of Zion) movement with its crude and inadequate methods of Palestinian colonization. There he laid the foundation of his philosophy which became known subsequently as "Cultural Zionism", and named after him "Ahad Haamism".

Later, when Theodore Herzl appeared upon the scene, Ahad Haam became the foremost antagonist of his "political Zionism". If this did not help to increase his popularity, for the masses of oppressed Jewry in Europe welcomed Dr. Herzl as a saviour, it served to fasten the public's attention upon Ahad Haam as the fearless critic who wielded a powerful pen and proved himself a most able logician. Herzl and Nordau, from their literary heights in Vienna and Paris, found themselves forced to take note of the strictures of the man from Odessa and to defend their position. Thus the nom de plume "Ahad Haam", which he employed in his very first article to indicate how unpretentious he felt and how little store he laid by his literary effort— for it means "one of the people"— actually came to signify the "one and only" man of his type in the literary guild, and he who entered the arena as a mere casual guest, became a fixed and permanent luminary, but one which most of the time shed light rather than warmth. Like a skilled surgeon, he wielded his scalpel mercilessly regardless of the pain it inflicted upon the patient.

To us, the younger school of Hebrew writers, Ahad Haam became, apart from his philosophy, the adored creator of a new style, one which cleansed the literature of its "Batlanut" (slovenliness), as it was called, and introduced in it a new and refreshing trend. He showed us that one could write Hebrew without the use of *"melitza"*—an over-abundance of Biblical phraseology. Hebrew was a living tongue which, though unspoken for many centuries, was yet throbbingly alive. It had never stopped growing and enlarging its vocabulary, as is evident from the Talmud and Midrash and the works of the mediaeval poets, Kabbalists and philosophers. Ahad Haam demonstrated how gracefully one could write Hebrew if one but knew how to exploit all of its resources. Needless to say, his example found many followers and imitators.

I am somewhat off my course, since my object here is not so much a study in literature or in Zionism as a delineation of Ahad Haam's personality. But one cannot write about him without appraising his role as a writer and philosopher of Zionism. To come back to my first meeting with him— it took place on a Friday evening, on the very day we landed. Before we reached Liverpool I sent him a Marconigram from the boat informing him that we would be in London that afternoon, and asking when we could come to see him. Upon arriving at our London hotel we found his telegraphic answer, welcoming us to England and inviting us, if possible, to be his guests at that evening's Sabbath meal. Notwithstanding that I knew I could easily get to his place by taxi, I telephoned him to inquire the location of his house—the temptation to speak to him was too great, knowing I was so near to him. Through the receiver I heard a clear and well-modulated voice, speaking slowly and in good grammatical English, but with a strong accent, instructing me to take the Underground near our hotel and change at Charing Cross for the station nearest to his place. A taxi, he said, would be easier, but would be expensive owing to the great distance from the hotel. I thanked him for this advice, which we did not follow. American spendthrifts that we were, and honey-mooners at that, we went by taxi.

The thrill of speaking to him from our hotel room was among the things that lingered in my memory of that European tour. I was impressed with his fatherly interest in advising us in detail how to get to his home, and it conveyed to me the idea that he must be a very cordial sort of man. On this point I was to be disappointed. The Asher Ginzberg I met that evening, while courteous and friendly, did not seem particularly cordial. He may even be said to have been somewhat cold and distant. Later on in our relationship I had cause to change my mind on this score. His apparent coolness with strangers—and that, after all, I was to him—was a kind of mask that hid the real man. It was part of his mentality which was inclined to look at the world through the glasses of stern logic. A Talmudist, he was also probably influenced by the dictum of the sage who taught that one should both "respect and suspect" a man, at least until he knows more about him. His seeming coolness was in large part studied and calculated. But behind this facade of apparent indifference as I found out in the course of the years, there stirred a warm soul with a lively and sympathetic interest in men and events. This is confirmed by his many letters, written to me and to

[7]

hundreds of others, which fill six volumes published during his lifetime.

Perhaps it is incorrect to speak of "coolness" in describing him. It may have been a kind of state of mind, a critical attitude which was constitutional with him. The fact that he was so much older than I—he 53 and I a mere stripling of 28—and so prominent, may have had something to do with his attitude. It may also be that the state of mind was not his but my own, that I imagined things that were not there. The sense of awe I felt in the presence of the master made me believe that there was a partitioning wall between him and me which neither of us had the right to seek to circumvent. There was also another circumstance which helped create this impression. He was a very poor conversationalist. He would listen rather than talk, and when he did talk it was rather cautiously, as if to make sure he would only say things he would have no cause to regret. He would think before committing himself. As a result, my conversation with him that evening lagged somewhat, on my part because I was a stranger and for the first time facing my adored master; and on his part because that was his habit. But I am a little ahead of my story.

Our taxi halted in front of 12 Glenmore Road, in what looked like a quiet and well-ordered neighborhood. The house was brilliantly illuminated and when we entered we saw the Sabbath lights burning. This sign of religiosity seemed somewhat at variance with Mr. Ginzberg's unorthodox attitude towards Jewish observances, as I soon had occasion to learn. It was evident that it was Mrs. Ginzberg who attended to the religious side of the ménage, and supervised the dietary requirements as well as the Sabbath rituals to which her husband, himself indifferent about such matters, gave silent assent. Our arrival was somewhat late, and the family and guests were already seated at the table. There were wine cups alongside the dishes, and I was wondering if Kiddush had been recited. I regretted our lateness, as I would have given half a kingdom to hear Asher Ginzberg chant the Kiddush—if indeed he did it.

Both Mr. and Mrs. Ginzberg greeted us at the door with a few friendly words as we entered, and indicated our seats at the festive board. Opposite us I saw the familiar face of a fellow-American, Professor Israel Friedlander of the Jewish Theological Seminary, who was then spending his vacation in London. (Many years later, at the end of the first World War, he met a martyr's death at the hands of bandits in the Ukraine, whither he went on a mission of mercy to bring American Jewry's relief funds to the po- grommised Jews of Russia.) There were two or three other guests, but I do not recall who they were. Of the Ginzbergs' three children only one was present, their daughter Rachel, who had returned from her studies in Switzerland only that morning. Madame Ginzberg, a tiny lady, talkative and on her feet most of the time, looked after the service and en- couraged each of us to partake freely of the tasty dishes which were passed around. My wife and I needed no special urging after the ten-day trip on the ocean with the dull boat fare. The conversation at the table moved at a lively pace. Dr. Friedlander, a handsome young man with a jet black beard which lent him an air of great distinction, was the leading spirit and told many Jewish stories and anecdotes. Mrs. Ginzberg took an active part in the table talk. She spoke exclusively in Yiddish, and I suspected that she had not yet acquired a sufficient knowledge of English to converse freely in it. All the others spoke either Yiddish or English, and occasionally one could hear a remark in Russian. Asher Ginzberg, who sat at the head of the table, and occasionally smiled at this or that remark, himself spoke very sparingly. To his wife and daughter he spoke in Russian.

In reality, the little man with the shiny dome, at the head of the board, who seemingly had so little to say, dominated the gathering. Consciously or not, everybody felt that the evening was his, the master's, and that they were all there chiefly because of him. His very reticence helped to create an atmosphere of reverence. He looked very distinguished with his carefully trimmed goatee and his neat attire. I believe I would have recognized in him a leading figure had I, not knowing him, seen him in a large crowd. His demeanor was that of a person of eminence, and not because he put on airs. Actually he was a very meek man, with a modest self-appraisal and with much charity in his appraisal of others. Yet he possessed a sense of self-importance which came to him from his awareness of the responsibility which the times had placed upon his shoulders. Involuntarily he found himself at the head of a great moral and spiritual movement, a teacher whose task it was to point out to his people the art of thinking clearly and of writing lucidly. This ingrown sense of responsibility influenced first of all himself. It taught him tameness and the need of self-control in what he said or did. In a certain measure he became an ascetic, though by nature he was quite fond of life and of the good things which life had to offer. There is not the least doubt that Ahad Haam was first and last a great moral personality. His fame as a thinker and writer rested primarily upon his character, and this was really his one great achievement in the realm of modern Hebrew culture. He brought into the Hebrew movement, together with his literary talents, the spirit of truth-seeking, good manners, and rigid ethical standards. He came at a time when such standards were sadly lacking. Neo-Hebrew came up of itself, as a necessary result of a number of factors, and its protagonists were often men unschooled in the ways of the world and ignorant of the amenities of camaraderie and of the ties which a common cause imposes. Not a few of these writers were wont to regard each other as competitors in the race for a seat in the temple of immortality—which was about all they expected out of their scholarly labors. Ahad Haam taught his colleagues to be decently human towards each other, even as he taught them to use Hebrew clearly and succinctly, without unnecessary phraseology and undue quotations which often only beclouded the meaning of a sentence.

These and other thoughts about him, as I jotted them down subsequently in my note book, flitted through my mind as I faced him that evening. His halting conversation afforded me a little time to appraise him and to pass in mental review his position and his moral worth. I recalled a statement he once made in a letter he had written to me in 1901, which revealed the highly ethical concept of life by which he was dominated. In that letter (it appeared among others in the second volume of his "Igrot" or letters, and is also quoted in full in Sir Leon Simon's volume: "Ahad Haam, Essays, Letters, Memoirs", Oxford, England, 1946, pp. 304-5) which was in answer to a request I had made, he gave a sketch of his life, described his studies and the manner in which he became a writer, and also his experiences as a merchant. Of the latter he writes: "In 1895 I lost my money in an unfortunate transaction" and then he adds parenthetically, "but thank God I defrauded no one". This was not mere boastfulness, a case of posing by one who wants to place himself in a favorable light before the world, but was characteristic of the man. To him, uprightness and genuineness were of supreme importance. In his insistence upon the ethical behaviour of human beings he first and foremost subjected himself to the moral code he imposed upon others.

As already hinted, Ahad Haam was not much of a "social lion". I do not recall that at any time that evening he attempted to lead or even to make conversation, and though he occasionally smiled I do not remember hearing him laugh. The truth is that there was something lugubrious about him; there emanated from him a sadness such as envelopes those who carry a heavy burden of responsibility. I then thought: Perhaps such is the case with all eminent thinkers, especially one like Ginzberg who was not merely a logician but in large measure also a Jeremiah, a bewailer and an accuser, whenever he delved into such questions as the "tragedy of the Jews" and the "tragedy of Judaism" (themes he dwelt on in his essays). At the bottom of it all he gave the impression of a lack of faith in the correctness or the ultimate triumph of the very values which meant so much to him, such as the revival of Hebrew and the renascence of the Hebrew nation in Palestine. His criticism of the means and methods employed in the cultural as in the colonizing work contained not a little scepticism about the entire Palestinian enterprise. Can a Jeremiah laugh? But on this point I had cause to change my mind a short time after our London visit when I met in Paris another eminent and fearless thinker, no less a man than Max Nordau. Nordau, too, delved into the problem of Jewish travail and he, too, was a bewailer and an accuser. His eloquent addresses at the Zionist congresses in which he depicted the cruel lot of the Jewish masses in Eastern Europe were so lurid and pathetic as to sway and bring to tears most of his audiences. Yet Nordau also knew how to laugh heartily, and that was one of his fascinating characteristics.

Dinner over, we all mounted one flight of stairs to Mr. Ginzberg's study, a spacious room well stocked with books. Ginzberg seated himself at his desk, and automatically we formed into two groups of males and females. My wife was drawn into the latter while the men clustered about the head of the family. At first the conversation was general, but before long that too was split up into two categories, according to the particular tastes and interests of the two sexes. I remember hearing Rachel Ginzberg complain of the hard trip she had had that morning when crossing the much-dreaded Channel; nearly all of the passengers were seasick. Madame Ginzberg inquired of my wife about conditions in America. We and Mr. Ginzberg soon found our own themes of discussion, in the course of which he inquired about my rabbinical work (I was then rabbi in Meridian, Miss.), and what, if anything, I was writing then. I asked him if he had the latest issue of the London *Jewish Chronicle* which I wanted to see, and his reply was that while he was a subscriber to the paper it was read mainly by his cook, who was a Jewish woman—and he sent his daughter into the kitchen to fetch it. This was the only anecdote I heard from him that evening.

Suddenly we heard Madame Ginzberg ejaculate in Yiddish: "Zeht, zeht, zei zeinen doch Chossen-Kalleh" (Look, look, why they are newly-weds!), continuing: "Here they are, spending an entire evening with us, and never a word Mazel Tov!" She referred to my wife and myself. Under pressure of questions by the hostess and the other women they elicited from my poor bride the "secret" of our marriage only some ten days before and that we were in England on our honeymoon, and Mrs. Ginzberg could not restrain her feminine enthusiasm. Everybody congratulated us, and Mr. Ginzberg smiled his usual detached smile.

I produced my little autograph book and asked him to write something. He took out his fountain pen and began to make preparations as if in the process of undertaking a task of great importance. He ruminated for a couple of minutes, knit his high forehead, and then slowly indited in his clear and lovely Hebrew handwriting five words which meant: "In memory of our pleasant meeting". Signing it in both Hebrew and English, he handed me back my book with an air of relief as though he had just completed a highly responsible piece of work. The following week, in Paris, when I handed the same booklet to Max Nordau, he scribbled quickly in English without apparent hesitation a sentence which contained a whole sermon and even a text for its basis: "All Israelites are brethren. Woe to them if they forget this apophthegm of their fathers". It is clear that philosophers, too, differ from each other in the tempo of their thinking and acting.

Late that evening we took our leave, and back to the hotel we went by the Underground, Ginzberg and Friedlander accompanying us to the station. Twice more, during our stay in London, we met Asher Ginzberg, once on an afternoon when he came to see us at our hotel and stayed for "Five O'clock Tea", and the last time when we again paid him a visit to the house at 12 Glenmore Road, a day before we left for Paris. But none of these meetings compared in thrill and excitement with our very first visit that Friday evening at the Sabbath meal.

But I was destined to see him once again, long after that London trip, and this time in Palestine, in 1925. This meeting took place under wholly different and more tragic circumstances, and it was quite unexpected. And the Asher Ginzberg I saw this time was a wholly different man, greatly aged and sickly, a bare shadow of the strong and alert man I had known in London in 1909.

In the 16 years' interval, many things had happened which placed their unmistakable stamp upon him and made him a broken man. The First World War with the untold suffering it brought upon millions of Jews in Russia, Poland and other lands had a crushing effect on him. I had already sensed his sufferings from a letter he had written to me dated June 26, 1919, in which he said: "As for me, the events of the recent past have shattered me, and I got to a point where I hate this devouring beast which regards itself as the supreme of all creatures. There are times when I feel like protesting to God for letting me live to see man's downfall and the desecration of all the moral values to which I had devoted my thinking and my love all through life" (published in the sixth volume of his "Letters", Tel-Aviv, 1925). He was also profoundly shaken by a domestic tragedy. His beloved daughter Rachel, the one I had met that Friday evening in his London home, married a Russian in Switzerland, where she pursued her studies. For him, the proud Jewish nationalist, who was so outspoken in his opposition to any and all forms of assimilation and especially to inter-marriage, this was a devastating blow from which he never recovered.

Such was the state in which I found him that summer of 1925 at the Herzliah hotel on top of Mount Carmel. Our meeting occurred under somewhat dramatic circumstances. I had no inkling of his being at that hotel when I went there soon after landing in Haifa. It was a terribly hot day such as one experiences in Palestine at that season, and I felt compelled to seek shelter and rest in my room. Around 6:30, when the guests were getting ready for the evening meal, I made my way to the veranda to get some fresh air before joining the others in the dining room. Seeing a vacant chair I sat down and enjoyed the beautiful panorama of the harbor and the lofty Carmel, one of the loveliest sights in all of the Mediterranean Basin. Then I surveyed my surroundings and started to note the men and women in whose midst chance had thrown me. As I turned to look at the man seated next to me I thought he looked familiar. A second look convinced me it was Asher Ginzberg. Beside him was Mrs. Ginzberg holding his hand. I greeted them and at first there was a look of strangeness in their eyes. Then they recalled me and seemed glad to see me again. But what a terrific change in the man! Thin and shrunken, he looked even smaller than he was. He held out a tiny hand and smiled his old detached smile which his eyes hardly reflected. Happy as I was over the unexpected meeting, I was painfully affected by his appearance.

For four days I lived under the same roof with him, and was an eye-witness to his state of exhaustion and enervation. He was chronically ill with arterio-schlerosis, and tried hard to hide his sufferings from others; but it availed him little. His morale was low, he could no longer work, and as he stated in a letter to Dr. Simon Bernfeld at that time: "Without work life has no meaning". Surrounded by friends and admirers, many of whom came to see him from different parts of Palestine, their solicitude only made him feel his uselessness all the more, and that his own world had passed him by. I would keep him company at the dinner table or on the porch, and had it not been for his wife, who was still as talkative as in the good old days, I would have had little or nothing to say to him, for now he was even more reticent than formerly. To carry on a conversation with him under the circumstances was most difficult. From time to time I could hear him heave a sigh.

My last glimpse of him was on the morning I left for Jerusalem. I spent a little time with him on the veranda, and managed to train my camera on him and snatch a picture which is one of my cherished mementos. He rose to pose for me, leaning heavily on his cane. As I entered the waiting automobile and the vehicle began to move I called to him: "Shalom, Mar Ginzberg". He waved his hand and his colorless eyes reflected a deep sadness.

Two years later, in 1927, when again in Eretz Yisroel, I visited him once more, but this time at his eternal resting place in Tel-Aviv's old Jewish cemetery (to distinguish it from the new burial place of the city). He passed away in his seventieth year, some sixteen months after our last meeting. Silently I stood with bowed head by the little mound which as yet had no tombstone but only a marker bearing his name. The tiny hill encased the earthly remains that once served as a shrine for a great and potent spirit. Years later, when standing in a Berlin Jewish book store examining the latest Hebrew publications from Palestine, I casually picked up a volume which conveyed to me posthumous greetings from Asher Ginzberg. The book, "Pirke Zikhronot" (Chapters of Reminiscences), bearing the imprint of Tel-Aviv, 1931, contained his interesting memoirs and also a number of letters he had written since the publication of his collected correspondence already referred to. The very last letter, written shortly before his death, was addressed to me. I had never received it, perhaps because he or his family failed to mail it, or because it got mixed up with other documents and was overlooked until it came to the attention of the editor of the volume. Among other things he states there: "What can I write you, aside from thanking you for your good wishes? Would that they come true if only in part. At present my condition is still bad and my hope of regaining my strength is growing ever smaller. But what is one to expect from a sick old man? I send herewith my blessing to yourself and your dear wife that you may live and keep up your work for many more years. Do inform me from time to time about your affairs and activities, and be not too exacting about the letters you get from me in reply to yours".

In 1935, when I again came to Palestine, the first thing I did in Tel-Aviv was to visit his grave. This time I found there a fine looking monument. It had, if I remember correctly, no special epitaph and no encomium about the distinguished departed. Only his pen name stood out in large Hebrew characters: A H A D H A A M , one of the people.

In the grateful memory of his people, to whose moral guidance he gave himself so eagerly and lovingly, he will ever remain the one and only, the unique and irreplaceable tribune, thinker and teacher. And his fame and influence promise to grow even more with the passing of the years.

Max Nordau

WITH MAX NORDAU I spent not more than an hour and a half that unforgettable summer of 1909, when my wife and I went through Europe on our honeymoon. But those ninety minutes were the high-water mark of our entire trip to the old continent, and served as a source of inspiration through all the years that followed. After that conversation with one of the outstanding thinkers of the period we felt like having caught a glimpse of a new horizon of the existence of which we had but a very faint idea.

Coming to Paris straight from London and the meeting with Ahad Haam, this visit to Nordau was particularly refreshing and stimulating. For truth compels me to state that I left London a somewhat disillusioned man. The sparsely-talking Ahad Haam, who measured everything with the yardstick of cold logic, and who evinced little enthusiasm even for the values which he staunchly championed—altogether, enthusiasm was at no time a part of his nature—this man who delved into the problem of Jewish pain and suffering like a master surgeon probing with his scalpel into his patient whom, indeed, he is eager to save, but who nevertheless does it with the objectivity of the professional specialist —Ahad Haam instilled into me a measure of pessimism about the Jewish future and the hopes centered in Palestine. His critical attitude had a somber effect on my youthful exuberance, and London's summer skies became overcast for us. I was still young enough to need encouragement in the ideals I believed in, and this I did not find in the house at 12 Glenmore Road. I was therefore glad to exchange the heavy atmosphere of England for the laughter-filled French capital. Max Nordau well symbolised the difference between the two cities. Contact with him had a tonic effect upon my drooping spirits.

I confess that when I started for Europe I had not the least idea that I would meet Nordau. It was remotest from my mind to seek him out for the purpose of spending a goodly part of an afternoon in a discussion of Jewish problems. With Ahad Haam the case was different: On him I had a certain claim as my editor and literary monitor with whom I had many things in common. But none of the ties which bound me to Ahad Haam linked me to Max Nordau. I knew that Nordau had come into Jewish life and leadership, like Theodore Herzl, from the outside, that he had been a thoroughly assimilated Jew prior to his becoming a Zionist, that, indeed, his very Jewishness was unknown and unsuspected before a startled Jewish world learned of his association with the author of "The Jewish State" in the political Zionist movement which they both launched. All this had much curiosity for me, to be sure, but very little else. I also knew that Nordau was a very distinguished physician and moral reformer who wrote weighty books on the foibles and moral degeneracies of the times, the vagaries, shams and hypocrisies of late 19th century Europe—books which placed him in the front line of the iconoclasts of all ages. All this would have made me hesitate to ask for an appointment with a great and very busy man.

It was Professor Friedlander of New York, whom I met that Sabbath night at the home of Ahad Haam, who influenced and encouraged me in that direction. On the way to the Underground to which we were escorted by both Friedlander and Ahad Haam, the former suggested that I go to see Nordau upon our arrival in Paris. When I stated my doubts about Dr. Nordau caring to receive me in view of his busy schedule, Friedlander assured me that Nordau would be happy to welcome me and my wife at his home, that both he and his wife were very hospitable people and that he was particularly interested in Jewish persons coming from America.

Thus reassured, I wrote to Dr. Nordau on the morning after we got to Paris. His answer came *express* (special delivery) that same afternoon. He would be very happy to see us, he wrote, and designated 5 P.M. of the next day as the time of the visit. He wrote a correct English, and the tone of his words was very friendly. This and the promptness of his reply set us at ease as we prepared ourselves for the event with much anticipation. Promptly at the appointed hour we arrived at the house on Rue Henner, No. 8, where we knew that a prominent and highly interesting man was awaiting us.

I consider it very fortunate that so many details of that visit remained fresh and fixed in my memory to this day. I had the foresight of keeping a note book of our trip—a habit I have assiduously cultivated ever since on the many trips I have made subsequently and for which I am grateful. My memorandum of that afternoon contained the salient features of our conversation and also my impressions of the man and his environment. A week later, in Berlin, I used it as the basis for an article which I sent to the *American Israelite* of Cincinnati. (It was also incorporated in my Hebrew book of Essays and reminiscences, "Yisroel B'Amerika", which was published in Tel-Aviv in 1928.) The present essay is based largely on the notes I jotted down that afternoon immediately after our return to our hotel. To us, who know what has happened to the Jews of Europe in the past generation, the words of Max Nordau, spoken

40 years ago, have a genuinely prophetic ring. And since I am using the word "prophetic" I ought to state that it is a most fitting description not only of what he said but of the man who said it. I cannot conceive of any one answering the description of a prophet, to the best of our imagination, better than Max Nordau.

Indeed, the man Nordau impressed me no less than his message, and I want to describe him as he still stands in my memory. But first a word about the surroundings in which I found him. He lived on the first floor of a typical Parisian apartment house of those days. To reach it one had to pass through a court yard which was embellished with a little flower garden. In response to our ring the door was opened by a smiling maid who conveyed us into a salon or reception room. I remember that I wondered whether it was the room in which Dr. Nordau the physician received his patients. It did not have the look of a professional waiting room such as we are accustomed to in the United States— no illustrated magazines for the patients to while away their time while waiting for their "next". But there were many books on a variety of literary and scientific topics. Everything about the chamber had the appearance of modesty, with no trace of showiness or luxury. The thought flitted through my mind: Was Nordau a rich man, and was the modest appearance of the place merely an indication of the proverbial conservatism and parsimony of the European well-to-do—so greatly in contrast with the spendthrift propensities of us Americans? The furniture, the pictures on the walls, the rugs on the floor—all bore testimony to a well-ordered and well-grounded life, but it also spoke of age. I thought that the female portraits on the wall must be of his wife and daughter. I also saw there pictures of Nordau himself in several poses, both photographs and drawings by

artists. In a corner of the room I also saw a sculptured bust
of the author of "The Conventional Lies".

Here I was struck with the contrast between Nordau and
Ahad Haam. In Asher Ginzberg's London study I saw no
pictures on the wall. If there were any I do not recall
them, or may be they were so few and inconspicuous that
they made no impression. Perhaps pictures belonged to those
"little" things of life which held no appeal for the earnest-
minded Russian-Jewish intellectual. In Nordau's reception
room, where we were seated, the pictures of himself and
family occupied places of honor. It evidently was part of
"this-worldliness" which had such a prominent place in his
outlook upon life. Quite likely it also was part of the optimism of his nature. Nordau was no ascetic, and if he
believed in loving one's neighbor it did not mean that one
must hate himself in the process. This thought, too, I carried
away with me from that afternoon's conversation.

After a wait of a few minutes we were invited into
Nordau's study. Advancing to meet us was the man I knew
so well from his pictures: a stocky person, not tall but
strongly built, his full-rounded face surrounded by a beard
nearly all white, his temples and cheeks marked by many
wrinkles. He seemed at that time in his late fifties or early
sixties. The most impressive part of his physiognomy were
his eyes which looked at me penetratingly yet kindly from
under their bushy brows. His was, on the whole, a thoroughly Jewish face, one might say a traditionally rabbinical face,
except for the beard which was too well-trimmed, too "aristocratic" to meet the requirements of the old-style rabbi. A
friendly smile played on his lips as he held out a large
heavy hand and bade us sit down.

During our conversation I took time to observe as well
as I could the arrangements of the room in which we found

ourselves. I then thought that a man's work room is part of his being, and that this is particularly true in the case of a thinker or an artist who spends there the larger part of his time working on or planning his creations. Dr. Nordau's study, where he worked on his books or articles, was not a large chamber. The few pieces of furniture it contained were of the cheaper sort, and they, too, showed age and the hard work to which they had been put in the course of many years. To me they appeared in the light of the indescribable charm that hovers over all things associated with great men or important historic events. Nordau's workroom told of a mind that labored ceaselessly, of an abundance of energy, of spiritual exertion, and of self-control. It also told of the satisfaction which comes to the morally strong. All around me were books, in the open cases along the walls, on tables and even on the floor, books in many languages and dialects, and also portraits and pieces of sculpture. On his large and massive desk I saw a heap of books which were evidently of the latest literary vintage. Protruding out of the mass I saw a volume the title of which attracted me. It was a French version of Nahum Slousch's "History of Modern Hebrew Literature" which had just then made its appearance and was destined to bring its author much fame. On the wall nearest the desk was a good-sized portrait of Theodore Herzl.

Nordau's large and amiable eyes eloquently bespoke the welcome he extended to us. I believe, however, that it was his voice which revealed his true personality. It was a richly resonant, stentorian voice, well modulated and entirely subject to the man's state of emotion—and Max Nordau was a highly emotional man. We conversed in the main in German, and only now and then resorted to English. His English was far from bad. In both languages he spoke in a manner as if to make sure that every word would convey the intended meaning, and I got the impression that it was done because he was laboring under the notion that German was as foreign to us as English was to him. He was a good and patient listener. When my wife or I spoke he did not for a moment interrupt us. But once we finished he threw himself with marked zest upon his opportunity to present his viewpoint. And he spoke heatedly, often raising his voice as though he were talking not privately but from a public platform. One could easily see that Nordau loved to talk, and that, I am sure, was one of his chief characteristics. The world knew him as the painstaking and devoted physician and fearless thinker and writer. Actually, he was more than anything else the impassioned orator, endowed above all with the gift to sway and convince his audience. Seated opposite him I watched the nervous tension behind his words, the twitching and turning of his throat muscles as he sought to put his ideas across. It mattered not that we were only two; to him we were his audience and he wanted to convince us as though we were a multitude. He spoke not merely through words. His entire being seemed to speak along with the words that rolled off his tongue so glibly: the eyes which smiled or blazed with zeal or anger, and the hands which gesticulated with the arguments he was propounding.

I shall not reproduce his views here in detail—a summary of it I gave in my article in the *American Israelite* already alluded to. Briefly, let me say that he was greatly interested in all things pertaining to American Jewish conditions, and he kept plying us with questions about the new Jewish community then in the process of growth and development in the Western Hemisphere. He wanted to know more about the way the Jewish immigrants were adjusting themselves to the new conditions, and chided those who disapproved of the crowded Jewish quarters in America's large cities (it was the time of the Galveston experiment, which aimed at diverting Jewish immigrants from the Eastern coast). He regarded it as only natural and even praiseworthy that the newcomers should want to live with their own brethren where alone they could find sympathy and understanding. But even the American settlements, he believed, were mere palliatives that would not settle the age-old Jewish problem. He knew that even in the United States anti-Semitism was raising its ugly head and would become progressively worse with the increase of the Jewish population. Palestine alone he saw as the answer to the problem of the Jewish future. There is no hope for the Jews so long as they remain a scattered people and a helpless minority everywhere. As a people the Jews must have a home of their own, where as a majority they would be able to control their own destiny. Palestine alone offers such a home. How strikingly similar to the Zionist thinking of our own day! Even here he expressed his apprehension that the Zionists were failing to make full use of their opportunity to bring masses of Jews to Palestine. It was the time of the "Young Turk" regime in Turkey, and Nordau believed that as a more liberal group those rulers of the Ottoman Empire would prove more amenable to facilitating the settlement of Jews in their ancestral land, provided the Zionist leadership knew how to go about it. When I mentioned Ahad Haam's central thought of a "cultural center" in Palestine in place of the political Jewish State which to him did not seem feasible, Nordau frowned and called Ahad Haam a "Schwaermer"—an impractical dreamer.

(Many years later at the London Zionist Congress—it was shortly after the close of the First World War—Nordau dwelt on this same idea of a mass migration of Jews to

Palestine as he expressed in our interview with him. He wanted the Zionist leadership to take advantage of the favorable turn afforded the Zionist ideology in the "Balfour Declaration" by organizing without delay an exodus of hundreds of thousands of Jewish settlers from all over Europe to take possession of the land. He regarded the physical possession of the soil by the Jews as imperative for the establishment of their claim to the land, and felt convinced of the feasibility of his plan in view of the British Government's friendly attitude to Zionism in those years. The core of his thought was that the Jews could thus easily become a majority in the Palestine of both sides of the Jordan as against the Arabs who then numbered only a little over half a million population, and the way to Jewish statehood would thus be shortened. Had the Zionists acted upon his plan at what was undoubtedly a psychological moment for their movement, many of the tragic occurrences that followed might have been averted. The Zionist Congress, however, turned his idea down as impractical under the prevailing circumstances.)

We rose to go and Nordau rang a hand bell to let his servant know so she would open the door down below for us. As we were leaving he noticed that my wife was sniffling from a cold she had contracted, and the physician in him asserted himself. He gave her his professional advice not to neglect the cold, and to avoid draughts, etc. Once again the pressure of the big, heavy hand, his domestic hailed a passing taxi, and we were on our way.

There was an interesting sequel to this visit. After the publication of my Nordau article in the *American Israelite*, I sent him a copy of it. In acknowledgement I received from him a postcard which I shall quote here as it sheds additional light on the man's social attitudes, and particularly towards printed articles about himself. Dated September 12, 1909, the card reads:

Dear and Reverend Doctor:

Many thanks for the kind intentions that have I am certain, guided your pen. I hope you are broad-minded enough not to take offence at my confessing to you that I have made it an iron principle never to read impressions published about myself. A long experience has taught me that it is impossible for a visitor after an hour's contact with a stranger to grasp the real facts, even the purely physical, about him, so what he writes even if charming from a literary or gossiping point of view, even if animated by the most friendly and even enthusiastic disposition, must necessarily be inexact and irritating to the object who knows better and resents involuntary blunders. The only means, to my experience, of retaining a pleasant impression and souvenir of a visitor is not to read his utterances about oneself. Now, I wish to think of you and your charming companion of life with the greatest pleasure, and this dictates my conduct. With kindest regards, also to Mrs. Raisin,

Yours very faithfully,

M. Nordau

Him, too, I visited at his resting place in Tel-Aviv's old cemetery when I was there in 1935, and lingering at his grave for many minutes there came back vividly to my mind the details of the visit to his Paris home.

He sleeps not far from Ahad Haam, Shmaryahu Levin, Chaim Nachman Bialik and other Russian-Jewish intellectuals and Hebraists, men with whom he often broke a lance in the controversy over the Zionist ideology and the ways and methods to attain the goal they were all after, but whom he deeply respected for their earnestness and mental and moral acumen. Opponents in what they believed were vital matters of principle, they now are neighbors and united in death, all reposing in the bosom of the same sacred soil so dear to them and in the repossession of which by their people they saw the one lasting solution for Israel's two-thousand-year-old-tragedy.

Simon Bernfeld

LONDON, PARIS, BERLIN—these were the three important étapes in our wanderings through Europe that honeymoon summer of 1909. We, of course, visited many other cities like Brussels, Amsterdam, Haag, Cologne, Frankfurt, Mainz, Dresden, lured and fascinated by their museums and libraries, their picture galleries and botanical gardens no less than by their theatres and fine summer performances. But those three capitals held out a special charm and meaning for us because each of them became associated in our memory with one prominent individual: London with Ahad Haam, Paris with Max Nordau, and Berlin with Dr. Simon Bernfeld.

Chance played its part here, too, that Bernfeld should be the one Jewish celebrity I should be able to meet at a time when Europeans are so vacation-minded. Upon arriving in Berlin I attempted to meet other notables, too, men whom I knew from their writings, like Professor Abraham Berliner, noted historian, and Reuben Brainin, distinguished Hebrew literateur, who later settled in New York. Neither of them was in the city, however. Brainin's answer to my letter came from Wiesbaden just as we were about to leave Berlin, and Berliner's post card reached us in America. But Simon Bernfeld was in the city, and when we arrived at his home one lovely afternoon in late July, we found ourselves in a most friendly environment. He and his wife, a buxom, good-looking lady, received us with old-style Jewish hospitality: tea, preserves, and a variety of cakes baked by Madame Bernfeld herself. The Bernfelds were excellent

[31]

hosts, and the two hours with them in their apartment at 81 Goethestrasse made us forget our homesickness for New York and Meridian, Mississippi. But for me this kindly welcome had a special significance growing out of my great reverence for my host who was one of the outstanding Jewish scholars and writers of that generation.

Simon Bernfeld was then in his prime, about 49 years old (he was born in Stanislavov, Galicia in 1860). Not tall, with a stoutish figure and florid complexion, he impressed me as a man simple in his wants and expectations from life and with but few claims on the Jewish people whom he did so much to educate and enlighten through his writings. His native simplicity showed itself in his mode of speaking, which was slow, quiet and subdued with no attempt at posing or impressing any one. His best works, such as "Preface to the Scriptures" and "Book of Tears", were still to be written, yet even then he had already won fame as the author of some ten volumes in Hebrew and German. His field was the science of Judaism ("Wissenschaft des Judentums"), Jewish history and biography, Jewish Bible studies and Jewish archeology. He showed a passionate interest in everything pertaining to Jewish life past and present, and his books will forever occupy a niche of honor in our multilingual Jewish literature. The blindness which afflicted him in later years caused but little difference in his studies and creativity. He possessed a wonderful memory which served him well during the many years of perpetual darkness, when he had to use the services of a secretary. But at our first meeting he was enjoying the best of health, and his eyes served him well though they showed even then unmistakable signs of overwork.

In later years fate willed it that I should come in contact with this man perhaps more than with any other European

Jewish savant in Europe. The visit I paid him in 1909 led to a more or less intermittent correspondence. I would write him my impressions of his books or articles and he would always react in friendliest style whenever I sent him a book or essay I had published, sometimes showing his apprecia· tion of my work by writing a review of it in some Hebrew magazine. This exchange of letters became more frequent as a result of his blindness, which brought with it a decided deterioration in his economic situation. This took place in the early 1920s. When I learned of his plight in 1924, I got in touch with several of our leaders in the New York rab· binate, including Stephen S. Wise, Mordecai M. Kaplan and Hyman G. Enelow, and we organised a Dr. Bernfeld relief committee of which I was the secretary-treasurer. As the result of an appeal I sent out to rabbis and communal work· ers throughout the country I collected more than $2,000, which I remitted to him in several installments. It led to a renewal of correspondence which lasted until 1937, when he became silent, evidently because of the difficulties the Jews of Germany were experiencing in ever mounting vol· ume under the Hitler regime. Most of his letters, naturally, were in Hebrew, but not a few were in German. It all de· pended on whether or not he had a secretary to whom he could dictate in Hebrew. His very last letters to me were, from all indications, purposely written in German out of caution lest the Gestapo and the censor make trouble.

I shall yet return to his letters, many of which contained philosophical observations on life and on the Jewish position in the world. Apart from that, there is ever present the motif of gratitude. He never forgot what I did for him. He called it *pikuach nefesh,* a life-saving act, and often alluded to it in the conversations I had with him during the summers of 1925-1931 when I visited Berlin annually and never failed to pay my respects to him. To the last he continued living in the apartment at 81 Goethestrasse, in Charlottenburg.

All in all, Simon Bernfeld was a tragic figure. Born to very poor parents—his father eked out an uncertain living as a Hebrew teacher—he suffered penury and privation all of his early days. His mother died when he was seven years old, and his father, always in search of bread, had little time to give to his son's upbringing. Whatever education he acquired during those early years was auto-didact. Only occasionally did he receive any sort of systematic tuition from young men, themselves university students, when home for their summer vacation, who instructed the promising youth as a matter of *Mitzvah* (charity). Nevertheless, his father, so burdened with his own cares and problems, exercised a decided influence on his life as a Hebrew writer.

The father was a *Maskil,* a Hebrew intellectual, a follower of the Mendelssohnian school with its knowledge and its programme of emancipating the spirit from the superstitions of the mediaeval ghetto and of remaining true at the same time to the essential ethical values of Judaism. Hebrew was the vehicle for this preachment and the great Moses Mendelssohn himself made use of it in *Ha-Measseph* magazine which he and others established in 1784. For the *Maskilim* of Galicia, and later of Russia, Hebrew in the course of time became an object in itself. It became the height of ambition to be able to write secular poetry in the ancient sacred tongue, or to write treatises on "profane" themes in it. Young Bernfeld inherited from his father this love for Hebrew and this ambition to write in it. In his autobiography, which appeared in *Reshumot* (Tel-Aviv, 1926), he states: "It is quite likely that I am the only one among the Hebrew writers who was purposely brought up to be a writer". His father greatly encouraged him in this. From his 13th year he kept preparing

[34]

himself, making translations into Hebrew from German and Polish works, and also trying his hand in original compositions. Gradually he made his way into the Hebrew literary world of the late '70s. His articles and translations appeared in *Ha-Maggid* and *Maggid Mishne*. At twenty an opportunity presented itself to him which decided his life-course. Michael L. Rodkinson offered him an editorial post on his weekly journal *Ha-Kol* (The Voice) which he published in Koenigs-berg. The pay was niggardly, but Bernfeld accepted it avidly because it gave him a chance to get away from his little Galician town and to settle in a large city in Germany where he could attend the University.

After suffering great hardships for five years, Bernfeld obtained his Doctor's degree from the University of Berlin (1885). His fame as a scholar and writer was established by now and he was elected to the important position of Chief Rabbi of Belgrade, Serbia (now Yugoslavia), a post he re-tained for seven years. Then he resigned and moved to Ber-lin. Communal labors and the demands upon his time as a rabbi were not to his liking. As he once explained to me, in telling of his motive in abandoning a lucrative and highly honored position, a rabbi's time and energies are wasted on so many small and unimportant matters that he has hardly any time left for his studies. In Berlin he took up his march on the thorny road of a scientific writer. Despite the small financial returns, he was happy that he could devote himself wholly to study and writing. He labored on various literary projects chiefly in Hebrew, and his works were published by *Ahiasaf* and *Tuschiah* and later by Bialik's *Dvir*. He translated the Scriptures into German, a version which evoked the admiration of the critics, and prepared other works in that language. His economic difficulties compelled him to work very hard to earn a living for his family. He literally burned the mid-night oil for years and years on end until his eyesight became impaired. He sensed the tragedy which was about to overtake him and his friends, among them Ahad Haam, chided him for not taking greater care. But he went on with his work, without which he would have found life unbearable. He kept working in a race against time, until his vision failed completely.

The tragedy of his blindness was all the more tragic in view of the fact that it might have been postponed, if not averted, or at least reduced in extent, had he not been ill-treated and defrauded by his supposed friends among the Hebrew publishers. He dwelt on this in his letter to me dated the tenth of Iyar, 1925:

"In August of last year (1924) my son and I went to Liebenstein, to a famous eye specialist to whom many thousands of patients go every year for treatment and many of them get cured. I, too, wanted to try, in the hope that I might be helped. Because of one money-mad person who held up a sum of money quite large for one in my circumstances, I postponed my trip from week to week. When I finally got there the doctor told me that not much could now be done for me, and that I would lose whatever little sight I still had left if I failed to take the necessary precautions. This meant that I would have to remain in that city several months for treatment. My debtor persisted in his hard-heartedness, and for lack of funds I was compelled to return home after two weeks. And now the light of my eyes is completely extinguished, and there is no more hope for me".

On my visits to him, as I sat opposite the blind man listening to his sad tale, there would come home to me the full meaning of the cruel fate which overtook him. It meant to work in the dark, never to know for sure that his efforts were properly applied, that the one to whom he dictated would take his words down correctly. It meant that he would never have the satisfaction and the joy of beholding the children of his spirit—his books—when they were printed. In December, 1924, he wrote to me:

"You doubtless recall the first visit you and your dear wife paid me. Those were the days of much work, when I believed myself strong as a rock, and had no worry about the next day. Now I have grown old and my sight is gone. You cannot imagine how difficult my work is even in the technical sense. I am unable to read or write a single word. My very signature is not my own, but is a mere facsimile. Were it not for the powerful memory which I possess to this day I could not continue working for one single hour. My mode of living, too, is most difficult. It is impossible for me to take a single step outdoors unless some one of my household accompanies me . . ."

And still he went on with his work, and the wonder of it is that he was now more productive than ever! He prepared for publication his already mentioned monumental "Mavo L'Kitve Ha-Kodesh" (Preface to the Scriptures), and his three-volume "Sefer Ha-Dmaot" (Book of Tears), an anthology of all the *Kinot* and *Piyutim*, the elegies and funereal poems composed by countless and often nameless authors during the many centuries of Jewish martyrdom in Europe. He edited a collection of his Hebrew essays called *Bnai Aliyah* (Supermen), a critical study of great Jewish philosophers and Biblical commentators of the Middle Ages, and wrote numerous essays and book reviews for *Ha-Olam* and other publications. And repeatedly he told me in his letters of new literary plans and projects which "keep rolling in my mind". Under the date of Adar 10, 1925 (he nearly always used the Hebrew calendar in his date line) he wrote: "Now that I am old, I have got to be more than ever diligent in my work, and every day I keep repeating to myself: 'Say not I will study when time will permit, for that time may never come' ".

Tragic, too, were his last years, when he began to nurse the hope of quitting Germany and settling in Palestine. In this he was destined for great disappointment. The truth is that Bernfeld never took his Zionism too seriously; he never reached the logical conclusion which a Zionist must reach—as so many have reached in our own day—that he himself is included in the solution which Zionism offers and that he must therefore do what he can to settle in Palestine himself as soon as feasible. With all his hatred and contempt for the Germans, in whom he saw the inveterate enemies of his people, he was inordinately fond of Germany as a country. For him Germany was still the great center of *Kultur,* and the land of the magnificent Rhine and the beautiful and enchanting Black Forest. In our conversations he would often expatiate on the physical and topographical grandeur of Germany and on her great spiritual contribution to the sum total of the world's culture. He remained constantly grateful for the education he had received in Germany's great universities. He believed that Frankfurt on the Main was Germany's fairest city, and it seemed to me that he felt that way not only because it was in truth a city of great physical beauty, but also because it contained what was beyond a doubt Germany's finest Jewish community.

I am sure that Bernfeld would have been quite happy to have ended his days in his adopted German fatherland except for Nazism and its ugly physiognomy. Even though he, the blind old scholar, was left more or less alone by the Gestapo, he felt it impossible to go on with such an existence. He then began to consider seriously the idea of migrating to Palestine, and he mentioned these plans in the last two letters I received from him in the spring and summer of 1937. Despite his advanced age of 77, he still hoped to be able to continue his research and literary work in Eretz Yisroel. And here came the terrible disappointment. The hindrance to his departure for the land of Israel came not from the Nazi authorities, whose policy at that time was still to facilitate the exodus of as many Jews as possible and thereby collect a highly profitable exit tax. It was the Zionist leadership in Palestine that thwarted his hopes for entering that country.

It will be recalled that in 1937 there was as yet no British White Paper forbidding Jewish immigration to the Holy Land. All Bernfeld needed was a special permit for himself and his wife which could easily have been supplied by the Palestine Jewish leaders had they bestirred themselves. He wrote to the Jewish Agency officials and they delayed their answer and their help. When their reply finally arrived it was far from satisfactory. Too many conditions were laid down, too much hesitation expressed lest he and his wife become a public burden. Finally, when all difficulties were side-tracked and the Matz Foundation of New York was ready to finance the trip and guaranteed his maintenance in Palestine, and just as he was making ready to depart, his wife fell sick and the journey perforce had to be indefinitely postponed. The outbreak of the war in 1939 put an end to all his hopes for emigration. Bernfeld remained in Germany where he died a year or two later. It is not possible to establish the exact date of his death, for the report of it reached America long after it happened. Even then it was not certain that it was he who had died. As in the case of all other Jews, the Nazis clamped on him a special Biblical name, so that when the news was published that one Simon "Israel" Bernfeld had passed away, there were not many who realised that by it was probably meant none other than the distinguished Dr. Simon Bernfeld.

The last time I saw him was in the summer of 1931, on my last visit to the German capital. Since then I made four more trips to Europe, but each time steered clear of Germany which I knew had become a valley of the shadow of death for our people. In Basel in 1936 and again in 1938, right across the German frontier, I could literally smell the stench that arose from the holocaust perpetrated by a people that had reverted to its primitive savagery. My thoughts then wandered to my many hapless friends entrapped in the new barbarism, and especially to blind and helpless Simon Bernfeld.

It would, I believe, be a profitable undertaking to prepare an anthology of Dr. Bernfeld's views and ideas on many matters as expressed in his books as well as in his letters to the many persons with whom he corresponded in the course of many years. His sage observations are of value in themselves at the same time as they cast light upon his own personality as a man and a Jew.

The first thing that stands out for our gaze is his love for Hebrew to which he devoted all his life. According to his memoirs, the first to rivet his attention upon modern Hebrew was Sholem Yacov Abramowitsch, better known by his penname of "Mendele Mokher S'forim" whose works the elder

Bernfeld possessed. Simon Bernfeld relates that he read Abramowitsch's famous novel "Fathers and Sons" numerous times so that he knew it almost by heart. He was then not more than 12 years of age. It served to set him upon his course as a Maskil and a writer. The Galician Haskalah (enlightenment) atmosphere was dominated by such potent spirits of a hundred and more years ago as Joseph Perl, Isaac Erter, Nachman Krochmal, S. J. Rappaport and some minor luminaries who placed their stamp upon the Hebrew movement of their country and gave rise to a special school known as the Galician school or étape, prior to the great upsurge of the Hebrew movement in Russia. Eminent later products of the Galician school were men like David Neumark, Henry Malter and Mordecai Ehrenpreis, but they were all excelled by Simon Bernfeld whose industry and productivity, aside from his amazing scholarship, set a record in the young and rising literature.

The attitude towards Hebrew of the Galician Maskilim was one of the utmost reverence, and to become a writer in that revived tongue of the Scriptures was regarded as an unusual distinction to which only a few fortunate elite could attain. It was not a question of material gain, for those who nursed such aspirations well knew that the financial reward to be expected was meager in the extreme. Bernfeld, too, was well aware of this. Like so many others who followed the same course, he sought to secure his economic position by becoming a rabbi, and as we have seen he abandoned that calling when it interfered with his scholarly work and literary ambitions. Even so he could have gained both fame and fortune as a writer had he chosen to use German as his vehicle. But he purposely turned to the Hebrew.

From his reminiscences and letters one also gleans his warm-hearted attitude towards people. He never writes bitterly of those who took advantage of him and withheld the monetary reward to which he was entitled. So, too, is his stand on the social problems of his time to which he refers. He does not hate even when he condemns and deplores. In this spirit he describes the murder of Rabbi Abraham Kohn of Lemberg (1848) by fanatics who opposed him for introducing reforms in ritual and educational matters in that community. They stole into his kitchen and poisoned his food, as a result of which the rabbi and his youngest child died. For some reason the perpetrators of the crime were never caught. Some years later the fanatics added further insult to injury when they dug the rabbi's body out of its honored grave and flung it into a canal where it was found. Bernfeld comments on this: "Howsoever repugnant and repulsive this crime is in itself, it seemed even more so to me when a Hassidic devotee from Belz told it to me with such glee and gloating as if it concerned not a human body but the corpse of some animal".

Of his mother, who died young, he writes: "My father often told me of my mother's beauty. When she stood under the marriage canopy her face shone like the moon. She was an educated woman according to the standards of those times, was proficient in Hebrew, and when my father was away in Russia she would write her letters to him in that tongue. There abides in my memory a soul-stirring picture of my mother on the morning of *Tisha B'Av* when she sat on a low stool reading the *Techinot* of the day. Because she understood what she read she wept bitterly, her hot tears streaming down her cheeks and wetting the leaves of the book. I greatly deplore not having any more that book which was a memento of a Jewish woman bewailing her people's downfall. I am incapable of describing the impression that scene had made on me and how it influenced me all through life".

In his autobiography Bernfeld tells at some length of the fine character traits of the Jewish masses of Galicia as he saw them in his boyhood days, of their religious piety and fervent reverence for Jewish learning. His father devoted every Sabbath afternoon to teaching in the synagogue Midrash and Aggada to the laboring groups of the town, all of them of the poor and under-privileged section of the community. This he did, of course, voluntarily, as a matter of *Mitzvah.* One such afternoon he was surprised by them with the presentation of a fine bronze Menorah in appreciation of his efforts in their behalf. They had pooled together their pennies until they had enough to purchase the gift. When he remonstrated that he wanted no reward of any sort, they insisted on his taking it, saying that the *Torah* which they learned at his feet was worth incalculably more than the price of the Menorah.

But he was severe in his condemnation of Hassidism which had struck deep roots in his native land, and which had found its apologists and defenders among the Maskilim of the 1920's among them men like Martin Buber and S. A. Horodetzky. "I care not what one may say", he states, "to me it is plain that Hassidism has introduced into our Jewish world an ugly reaction. There now appear protagonists of this cult who speak favorably of its "Torah"—but what is this Torah if not boring and misleading? The legends which are used to adorn the deeds of the Hassidim are so many idle words that make no sense. All who are engaged in picturing Hassidism in bright colors are merely falsifying history and will be held strictly accountable for it".

So, too, is his verdict about Reform Judaism on the history of which he wrote an important volume ("Toledot Ha-Reformatzion B'Yisroel"). In a letter he sent me dated Ab 3, 1928, he states: "When I wrote my book on the Jewish Reformation I was fully aware of what makes the indispensable basis for every Reform, and why the Reform movement in Germany was a failure. Every Reformation must come about through a strongly religious urge and impulse, through religious ecstasy. Only then can it be positive and creative. Otherwise it means nothing more than a sheer throwing off of the burden of religion. But in order to throw off the yoke one need not resort to a Reformative action. That is mere anarchy which comes of itself . . . These many years I have been troubled by this problem: On the one hand religion to the Jews has become a degrading fetich, and on the other hand it is nothing more than anarchy . . ."

Bernfeld is very unhappy about the moral climate of the world which he saw as a result of Christianity's influence on the nations. He deplores the fact that after Christianity's sway of nearly nineteen hundred years, supposedly Christian nations still hate one another so fiercely and still resort to the bloodiest wars in their attempt to exterminate one another. Hence his pessimistic outlook for mankind generally and particularly for the Jews. When I sent him my Hebrew essay on the forces working for goodwill between Christians and Jews in the United States (1931) and on the efforts put forth here for a better interfaith understanding he expressed his reaction to it in a letter dated Erev Pesach, 1931: "You say that eventually truth will prevail and men will learn to live together in peace and brotherhood. I, too, hope so, but I fear it will take a very long time to realise. There never was a time when there were lacking among the Gentiles, too, noble-hearted men who sought to shield us with all their strength. This happened even in the days of the Crusades when Catholic Bishops placed themselves in the path of the murderous bands. So it is also in our day. But what can we do if man's moral progress is so slow that he makes one step forward and several steps backwards! In the last few years we have been standing on the brink of catastrophe. I believe that we are on the eve of a war the like of which the world has never seen. If such a war actually comes, it will devastate the whole world. We are in the habit of thanking God for having endowed man with reason, but it is that same gift of reason which man utilizes to invent weapons with which to destroy the world".

This was written in 1931, two years before the advent of Hitler and eight years before World War II. The blind and secluded Simon Bernfeld thus foresaw what so many open-eyed scholars and statesmen failed to see until too late . . .

In that same letter he also makes the following observation about the anomalous position of the Jewish people: "The situation of our people, which is scattered all over the world, makes me particularly sad. Our tragedy was demonstrated in the last World War (1). The nations of the world went berserk and attacked one another with terrible cruelty. Yet horrible as it was for Germans and Frenchmen to slaughter one another it is something understandable, since such is the order of the world. But that Jews should kill their fellow-Jews, German Jews those of Russia and vice versa, is more than just a case of insanity—it is an attack on nature itself. Apart from this the Jews of every warring country have turned this heart-breaking tragedy into a comedy —in the special effort they were making to convince their Gentile neighbors of their deep-seated patriotism. Thus did Rabbi Guedemann of Vienna preach on Sabbath Hannukah, 1915, that Jews are fighting in the war with all their hearts and souls because it is a 'sacred war'; they are fighting not for Austria alone but for themselves. The victory of Austria will mean the victory of the people of Israel. But on that very Sabbath Hannukah the London Chief Rabbi delivered a sermon in almost identical words but in the very opposite sense: The Jews of England (said he) are taking part in the war because it is a war for the sacred purpose of annihilating Germany and Austria. The victory of England will be the victory of the people of Israel . . ."

Finally I wish to add a few words about his book "Sefer Ha-Dmaot" (Book of Tears) which, as already stated, appeared in three volumes and contained the elegies (*Kinot* and *piyutim*) of the many generations of Jews who endured such a terrible martyrdom for remaining steadfast to their faith. The mere fact that Bernfeld undertook this work proves how deeply he felt in his own soul the fullness of his people's tragedy. He wanted to erect a monument to all those unnumbered and unnamed martyrs who preferred to immolate themselves upon the altar of Judaism rather than prove false to themselves. By collecting all the elegies and dirges they or their descendants have left us, he wanted the world to "hear their very voices, their sighs and outcries, their weeping and lamentations". "There does not exist the poet", he says further in his preface, "whose genius is equal to depicting the anguish expressed so fearfully in these records of our fathers. Yet out of these laments we also hear the voice of solace and of hope, assuring us that the Jewish people has never abandoned its belief in the eternal verities preached by the Prophets who foresaw an ideal future".

I do not know what happened to Charlottenburg-Berlin under the Allied bombings, and whether the house at 81 Goethestrasse is still standing. But if Germany ever retraces its steps to the ranks of civilised peoples, I would suggest that a tablet be affixed to the place with a legend somewhat like this: "On this spot there lived and labored for many years and decades the John Milton of the Jewish people, Doctor Simon Bernfeld, distinguished Hebrew writer and scholar, who despite his blindness wrought and created great and inspiring works. His own people and the entire civilised world are greatly in his debt and everlastingly grateful".

Nahum Sokolow

It is now a little over fifty years since I came in touch with Nahum Sokolow for the first time. It was contact by mail only. My personal acquaintance with the foremost figure of Hebrew journalism goes back to a much later date, to 1921, when I called on him at the Commodore Hotel in New York to invite him to address a Zionist rally in my home city, Paterson. He greeted me on that occasion as an old acquaintance and friend, reminding me of my collaboration with him on his *Hatzefirah*, the Hebrew daily he had edited in Warsaw, something I had well-nigh forgotten myself, and had something nice to say about my work as a Hebraist. He spoke a perfect English, with an accent which savored neither of Russian nor of German, but could best be described as an English accent such as a polyglot foreigner would acquire after a long-time residence in England. From the first he captivated me by his cordiality and his unmistakable refinement of speech and manners. Before me stood a highly cultivated gentleman of superior mental and spiritual attainments—which I knew him to possess—who yet seemed utterly unaware of it in his effort to make me feel at home with him in his hotel apartment. It was a visit I long remembered.

But my first contact with him, by an exchange of letters starting in 1897, though it grew hazy in my consciousness with the passing of time, played an important role in my life, for it had a decided influence on my cultural development. Like Ahad Haam a year later, Nahum Sokolow taught me the craft of writing by means of the work he com-

missioned me to do for his daily. It was not as exacting a
task as I was to perform later for Ahad Haam's *Haschiloah*
which, being a monthly and intended for the more discrim-
inating among the Hebrew readers, demanded much greater
care both in thinking and execution. Work on a daily paper
of the small dimensions of the *Hatzefirah* was of a simpler
character. All I had to do was to chronicle the events taking
place in the Jewish quarter of New York of those days and
send it to Warsaw.

It was by sheer accident that I got the idea of engaging in
such work. I was then a mere lad of less than 16 and dreaming of entering the Hebrew Union College to study for the
rabbinate. Much of my leisure time I would spend in the
reading room of the Educational Alliance, where I found a
collection of all the Hebrew periodicals published in various
countries in Europe and in Palestine. The *Hatzefirah* attracted me by its form and style, and as a boyish prank I
wrote to the paper offering my services as correspondent
from the United States. A month later I received a letter
written in Nahum Sokolow's fine hand. He gladly accepted
my offer and instructed me what and how to write. One
thing he forgot to mention, to me most important—my honorarium. Nevertheless I accepted the "position" of "chief
representative" of the great Hebrew daily *Hatzefirah* for all
of the Western hemisphere, and for many months faithfully
wrote a weekly letter which was printed after it was duly
corrected by Mr. Sokolow. For me it proved to be an excellent school for Hebrew composition and actually introduced
me into the world of Hebrew letters. My work on *Hatzefirah*
made possible my "promotion" to the *Haschiloah*.

My meeting with Mr. Sokolow in 1921 was a prelude to
many other meetings in after years when I would see him
at Zionist gatherings or in private homes, where he was

nearly always accompanied by his daughter, Dr. Celina Sokolow. I also encountered him at Zionist congresses in Europe. It was always the same pleasant experience. Nahum Sokolow possessed great social charm, was an excellent conversationalist, and possessed the gift of making people feel at home in his presence. Of all the Hebrew writers I have known, he was probably the most interesting. Maybe that was due to the fact that, famous as he was as a Jewish writer, he was really more than just a writer, more even perhaps than a Jew, even though he was so thoroughly steeped in Jewish learning and so ardently devoted to the Jewish nationalist cause. He was as true a "citizen of the world" as I have yet found.

An estimate of Nahum Sokolow's place in Jewish life I gave in a symposium about him published in the Hebrew weekly *Hadoar* of New York, on the occasion of his seventieth birthday. I quote a few sentences:

"How can we best describe this outstanding man? It is altogether too simple to say that Sokolow is a synthesis of many schools of thought, that he is a combination of East and West. At one and the same time we see in him the old-fashioned Talmudist and the man of modern culture, one who is rooted both in Jewish learning and in the world's best literature. He astonishes us with his rich and unique Hebrew style and with his elegant use of other languages in which he writes. He is a gifted orator and an original thinker. With uncommon success he writes poetry as well as prose, and though dominated by spiritual cravings, he is also a practical man. Half of his day he devotes to study and literary work, and the other half to important political activity, often visiting at the courts of kings, princes and Popes in behalf of

the Jewish nationalist revival. As a writer he is noted
for the multiplicity and variety of his efforts; he
writes stories and biographies, character sketches,
parables and critical essays. There is hardly a branch
of literary creativity at which he did not try his hand,
and always with marked success. The older he gets
the more ardent and ebullient become the spiritual
powers within him, and scarcely a day passes without
his achieving some worth-while thing or expressing
some important thought".

Then I come to the conclusion that even this characteriza-
tion barely suffices to do justice to Sokolow because we are
here dealing with what the world, for lack of a better term,
calls "genius". Sokolow was a genius not in any special
sense of an Einstein, an Edison or a Shakespeare who attained great fame in certain special fields, but by the very
many-sidedness of his gifts and talents, by his unusual ability to imbibe and absorb more and more knowledge, which
he instinctively uses in the right time and place to further
the causes dear to his heart. Others, who sought to give a
close-up of him reached a like conclusion.

The important thing to remember about him is that he was
all his life a devoted servant of his people. He served it as a
writer and he served it as a diplomat and political leader
when the mantle of Theodore Herzl and of Chaim Weizmann
fell on him. To serve the cause of Jewry he travelled far and
wide and he was as well known in New York as in London,
in Johannesburg as in Tel-Aviv, in Rome as in Buenos Aires.
The wonder of it all is that, with his vast erudition and his
thoroughly systematised knowledge, he was a self-taught
man. He never saw the inside of a high school or a university. Like all Jewish children of the Russian "Pale", Sokolow
was a product of the Cheder and the Yeshivah where he was

given a thorough grounding in the Bible, the Talmud and the vast rabbinic literature that emanated from them.

But he was a "wonder-child" from the very start. Learning came easy to him. As a youth, while still wearing the traditional *kaftan* and *peos* (side locks), he became emancipated from many of the superstitions and inhibitions of Jewish Orthodoxy. He took up secular studies without the aid of teachers, specialised in history and languages, and in a comparatively short time perfected himself to the extent of becoming one of the best informed minds in Europe and certainly among the Jews of Russia and Poland, whose mentor and literary teacher he was destined to be for a full generation through the medium of the *Hatzefirah*, of which he became the editor in 1885.

A few words about the part played by the Hebrew press in the enlightenment of Russo-Polish Jewry are in order here. There were some six million Jews in the Russian empire at the time of Sokolow's editorial activity, and their literary needs were supplied by two little daily newspapers, the *Hatzefirah* of Warsaw and the *Hamelitz* of St. Petersburg (now Leningrad). Here and there were also weekly or monthly publications in Yiddish like the *Volksblatt*, which also appeared in St. Petersburg, but for some reason these could put up but little competition against the Hebrew press. The mass of Russian Jewry of that period was not enlightened enough to feel the need of a newspaper in the Yiddish of their daily speech; that was to come later, at the turn of the century. But there was one group of people who were highly cultivated in Hebrew as a result of their traditional Jewish up-bringing. All male children (later on also girls) were sent to Cheder to acquire a knowledge of the Hebrew prayers, and many of them went much further than the elementary stage. These were the elite, the intellectuals who rose above the masses and despite their limited numbers exerted a considerable influence on their communities. It was to them that the two above-mentioned periodicals appealed because they supplied them with much-needed information on world affairs and, more especially, because they were published in the language which they all adored, the language of their own great past and noble literature, Hebrew.

There was something unusually daring in the mere idea of a daily newspaper in a language which no one spoke, which was "dead" to all outward appearances except for the fact that it was used as a "holy tongue" (Lashon Ha-kodesh) in the synagogue ritual. No other people was known to have attempted anything like it. Yet the "Maskilim" of Russia dared it, and notwithstanding their struggles and unequaled sacrifices which often resulted in failure, they ultimately succeeded far beyond their fondest hopes. It was due to the spade-work with the "dead" language in Russia and Galicia that Hebrew actually became fully alive and is today the spoken language of the hundreds of thousands of Jews of Palestine and of countless thousands in other lands. And in this remarkable Hebrew revival Nahum Sokolow played a noteworthy part.

Hatzefirah was a far more progressive publication than *Hamelitz* of St. Petersburg. It had the advantage of appearing in Warsaw, which then harbored the largest Jewish community in Europe, whereas St. Petersburg had a comparatively small number of Jews, most of them assimilated and russified. The greatest advantage of *Hatzefirah*, however, was in having Nahum Sokolow as its editor. He brought to his task not only his rare mental gifts and his rich fund of knowledge, but also a sense of reverence for his opportunity and of responsibility to his Jewish cause. Printed in Warsaw, the paper was circulated not only in the Polish capital but even more in the provincial little towns of Poland, Lithuania and the Ukraine where it was read, studied and commented on. There may have been but one or two subscribers in a town, but the paper passed from hand to hand, and its arrival was an event looked forward to by the people every day. When too poor to subscribe individually, several persons would often organise into a club, pool their few kopecks, and in that way raise the needed amount. Sokolow was their adored teacher. He almost single-handedly filled out the paper every day, writing on world politics, reviewing books, contributing scientific articles, and now and then even publishing a short novel of his own. A weekly feature he introduced was the "Feuilleton" which was a humorous observation on Jewish or general affairs. It appeared in the Friday edition of the paper and would thus supply light and enjoyable material for his Sabbath reading public.

In his day Nahum Sokolow was the ablest Jewish journalist. In addition to Hebrew he also wrote in Polish, Russian, German and English, and aside from his work on *Hatzefirah* also edited a weekly paper in Polish and was for many years a contributor to the London *Jewish Chronicle* and other publications in English. He had a speaking knowledge of the languages he wrote in as well as of French and Italian, and it was his linguistic accomplishments which made him so valuable a representative of Zionism in later years when he, as President of the World Zionist Organization, carried on negotiations with heads of many governments. But writing was his strongest point and greatest passion. Theodore Herzl said of him that he "possessed all of the basic culture of the modern age and conscientiously pursued the every-day events, proving himself a journalist in the best sense of the term". Another eminent Jewish literateur, Gustave Karpeles, characterised him as "the true and faithful journalist, a writer by the grace of God". Sokolow, however, was in truth much more than a mere journalist, howsoever distinguished. Much of his time he gave also to serious literary work and to scientific research, as is evidenced by the large number of works that poured from his pen, books on a variety of topics, on Antisemitism, on Palestinian geography, on Baruch Spinoza, on Zionism, on the Orthodox rabbinate. His three-volume work on outstanding Jewish personalities, like Walter Rathenau, Joseph Israels, Chaim Nachman Bialik, etc. is a veritable classic of appreciations such as only a great master could write. He wrote early in his career a text-book of the English language in preparation for the day when, as he foresaw, there would be a large Jewish migration to America, and he sought to help such prospective emigrants to learn English. He also made Hebrew translations of Herzl's *Alt Neuland*, parts of Graetz's History and other books. At his death, in 1936, he left behind a number of works in manuscript.

Hatzefirah, however, remained his first and last love, and though forced to abandon it in 1914, with the outbreak of the First World War when he was compelled to leave Poland, he always looked back longingly to that period of his usefulness when he edited a little four-sheet Hebrew daily for the small-town intellectuals in Eastern Europe. Once at a dinner-meeting in New York I heard him state that one of the cogent reasons that brought him to America was the fact that nearly all of his one-time readers of *Hatzefirah* had emigrated to the United States, and he came here in order to renew their acquaintance . . .

To go back for a moment to my first meeting with him at the Hotel Commodore in New York, I believe it characteristic of the man that he was so thoroughly democratic, never aloof from the people but always a part of them and glad and anxious to be with them and to have them with him. When I called on him that afternoon I found his ante-room full of people, many of them, no doubt, his old readers and admirers, others just idlers who came out of curiosity. They were all waiting for the great man to come out to them after he had attended to some important business, as they were told he was then engaged in. When I gave my name and told of my mission to one of the attendants, I was at once taken inside to a waiting room. After a few moments I was surprised to see Sokolow come out of his bed-room with traces of an interrupted after-luncheon nap still on his face. Smilingly he apologized that he had to have a siesta to rest from all of the banquets and dull speeches he was compelled to attend nearly every day. His afternoon nap, he said, was essential for his rest, for he was a very tired man, and that was the "important business" he was engaged in while the people in the ante-room were waiting. He had much to do, he continued, and then quoted in Hebrew: "The day is short and the work plentiful". When our interview ended, he accompanied me to the exit through the ante-room where his many fans rose to greet him reverently. On all sides hands stretched towards him with the words "Sholom Aleichem", and for each of them he had a friendly smile, a word of recognition, or a reminder of events long past in the far off days in Warsaw.

It was a scene such as one sees at a Hassidic gathering when the faithful cluster around their adored "Rebbe".

But I recall many other scenes: in Berlin, in 1928, at a Zionist rally, where he is the main speaker. His theme is a Talmudic dictum: "David, King of Israel, liveth". The speech is a truly Sokolowian effusion, a concatenation of philosophical observations and historical elucidations bearing on the Jewish future and Israel's survival as a people. From his lips roll ceaselessly parables, anecdotes, quotations from the works of the masters—all in a beautiful German. The huge audience sits breathless. Another time I see him in my own city of Paterson, in the large High School auditorium, where he is greeted by 1500 men and women. When I, as chairman, introduce him, he gets a tremendous ovation. He begins in English, but the audience protests. They want to hear him in Yiddish; others shout their preference for Hebrew. He suggests a compromise. For five minutes he harangues them in Hebrew and then goes over to Yiddish and carries on in that tongue for an hour and a half. At the end he is as fresh and fit as when he began. Another time I hear him speak before a Hebrew group at Cooper Union Hall in New York. His theme is *Ha-Ani Ha-Kibbutzi* (The Collective Ego) which he delivers in a masterly Hebrew in the Sephardic pronunciation.

I also remember him in a lighter vein, on a Friday night at the time of the Zionist Congress in Basel in 1931. After the Sabbath Eve meal and its accompanying atmosphere of peace and cordiality among the delegates, I see Nahum Sokolow in the large social hall of the hotel surrounded by many worthies from America and elsewhere, among them Stephen S. Wise, Abe Goldberg, Jacob Panken, Shmaryahu Levin. The heated debates over Congress issues are forgotten, and in their stead is a spirit of mirth and friendly discussion. Humorous stories from Jewish life are heard on all sides and each of the men in the group contributes his share. When it comes to Sokolow's turn he is in no way behind the others. Anecdotes, jests, funny tales pour from his mouth to the delight and delectation of an audience that by this time had grown to large proportions.

Born a "wonder child", Nahum Sokolow remained such to the very last.

Menahem Mendel Ussishkin

AMONG ALL THE LEADERS of Zionism I have known, Menahem Mendel Ussishkin was the one man whom I not merely respected but in a sense also feared. My fear of him was rooted in the aversion I have always felt for the dictator, the man on horse-back who commands and will brook no opposition and no difference of opinion. To me and many others Ussishkin was that kind of a man. He was so entirely different from the other great luminaries whom Zionism had brought to the surface of Jewish life. Theodore Herzl, Max Nordau, even Ahad Haam were chiefly theorists, groping through the maze of problems to find their way to the solution they had envisaged. Ussishkin needed no groping and no probing. He was always sure of himself; his way lay plain and clear before him. It was this very cock-suredness that made him an object of fear—and of envy—to many, though all respected and admired him for the boldness and firmness he displayed in his approach to the Jewish problem. He was by nature a leader of men, but a leader whose ways and methods would be unacceptable in a true democracy. He lacked the finesse and the subtlety of the democratic political leader.

His "dictatorship", if we may call it that, stemmed perhaps from the fact that he did not consider the Jews of his generation a full-grown people capable of knowing its own mind and of managing its own affairs. His great love for his people did not blind him to its faults, faults for which he held the Jews blameless, since they resulted from their thousand-year-long wanderings and tribulations, but which

[59]

were there just the same. Like Moses he beheld in them a generation of slaves who must be rescued in spite of themselves by those who were strong enough to lead them out of bondage. Because of his forceful personality he prevailed and succeeded where others failed, and at the time of his death he could point to achievements such as few Jewish leaders of our time could have boasted of.

An explanation of Menahem Mendel Ussishkin lies, I believe, in the circumstance that he was himself an eyewitness and a victim of the anti-Jewish excesses of Czarist Russia where he was born and brought up. He was a student of engineering at the Moscow university when there broke out the bloody pogroms against the Jews with which Alexander the Third inaugurated his reign (1881). It meant an end of whatever fond hopes Ussishkin and other enlightened Jews may have harbored of eventual emancipation for the Czar's six million Jewish subjects. For men like Ussishkin it was most irksome and galling to contemplate a future of perpetual rightlessness in their own native land. Indeed, those pogroms brought an awakening to the whole mass of Russian Jewry, even to those of them who were not entirely conscious of the full gravity of their plight. Something terrible has happened to make them sit up and take notice. Before the full gaze of a supposedly civilised world, men, women and children were butchered in cold blood and their belongings stolen or destroyed because they were Jews. Consciously or subconsciously, all began to feel that this Russian land of their birth was a cruel step-mother who did not want them, and that to remain there meant to condemn themselves and their children to endless poverty and misery. The more courageous among them decided upon emigrating to the mysterious far-away New World which was beckoning to them from across the Atlantic, and there and then began that tremendous hegira which transplanted millions of human beings from one continent to another and made possible the up-building of what is today the largest, wealthiest and most powerful community of Jews known to history.

Ussishkin belonged to what was then a very small minority of Russian Jewry that failed to see in the trend towards America a solution of the Jewish problem. His knowledge of Jewish history reminded him that there were other bright chapters in the story of his people which began like that of the United States. Jews once were powerful and even enjoyed self-government in Babylonia, there was a "Golden Epoch" in Spain, and at one time the Jews commanded much influence and even a form of autonomy in Poland. It all came to nothing. The periods of comparative peace and prosperity were followed by others in which Jew-hatred came to the fore accompanied by political outlawry at the hands of the governments and by rioting and killing at the hands of infuriated mobs. The so-called liberalism of the 19th century was proving a fiasco, for even in such enlightened lands as France and Germany Jewish emancipation was largely on paper only; in every-day life the Jew was being discriminated against as though there had been no French and American revolutions with their declarations on the dignity and rights of the human person. Would not the new chapter of his history the Jew was beginning to write in America be but a doleful repetition of his experiences in the Old World? Ussishkin and many others felt that one must take a long view of history. Not even the United States could insure safety and security for the Jews as a people. These they could find in their ancient homeland alone where they must themselves become a majority. Not America but Palestine would ultimately solve the Jewish problem. The slogan uppermost in the minds of the Palestinian-minded Jews of those days was "Auto-Emancipation"—the idea contained in the remarkable brochure published by Dr. Lev Pinsker of Odessa in 1881. Fifteen years later Theodore Herzl, who had never heard of Pinsker's pamphlet, reached the same conclusions in his "Jewish State", with which began the history of modern Zionism.

Because of his firm character and unshakeable convictions which tolerated no sort of compromise, Ussishkin soon became the recognised leader of the Jewish nationalist movement in Russia, then known as "Hoveve Tzion" (Lovers of Zion). He retained that leadership throughout his long and active life. When Herzl, Nordau and Zangwill appeared upon the scene and political Zionism became an established and deeply-rooted movement, they were joined by Ussishkin and many other prominent East-European leaders. But Ussishkin remained the conscience of the nationalist ideal who would not permit it to be vitiated and swerved from its one basic phase, its Palestinian orientation. If Jews are to be reconstituted into a nation, it can only be in the land of their national origin. Herzl himself never stressed Palestine strongly as the only land for the Jews. His "Jewish State" leaves that point blank. Not the land but the State is what matters, the political arrangement whereby Jews can establish themselves in a given territory as a self-governing entity. Palestine, to be sure, should be given preference, but if it cannot be had then the territory must be sought elsewhere. Herzl foresaw the difficulties that would have to be faced in connection with Palestine which was then a possession of the Ottoman Empire. He tried his utmost to induce the Sultan of Turkey to cede that piece of territory to the Jews. Unsuccessful in his negotiations with the Sublime Porte, he attempted to circumvent these difficulties by diplomatic interventions with some of the European Powers. He even went so far as to arrange a meeting between himself and the German Kaiser when the latter visited Palestine (1898). All these efforts proving abortive, and becoming convinced that Palestine was unattainable, Herzl launched his plan for a territory for Jews wherever that could be found. Under the spell of his impassioned appeal, the Zionist Congress in 1903 agreed to send a commission to examine the likelihood of Jewish colonization and ultimate statehood in various parts of the world then still uncultivated and sparsely populated, like El Arisch, Angola, Uganda. Thus arose what is known as the Territorialist movement. It had but a brief life, and nothing came of all its efforts. Menahem Mendel Ussishkin and his followers put up a strong resistance against Herzl. He convened a special Zionist congress in Palestine that same year of 1903, and another special conference in Charkoff, Russia, where he marshalled the full Zionist strength against the Territorialist scheme. Theodore Herzl found himself a leader deserted by most of his legions who hitherto had followed him blindly under the glamour of his personality. Less than a year later he died of a heart ailment said to have been brought on by this schism. It is certain that at that time Herzl was a broken-hearted man, if not because of Ussishkin's opposition, which hurt him deeply, then as a result of his realizing that his leadership thus far had failed and Zionism had reached an impasse from which it could scarcely extricate itself.

Ussishkin thus proved himself the strong man of Zionism, strong not only because he knew what he wanted but also because he knew the psychology of the people he was seeking to save. Their very suffering had made them amenable to his firmness and easily pliable to his doctrines. He never approached the Zionist problem with kid gloves; his was the categorical imperative. Not particularly gifted as a writer, he made up for it by his talents as a speaker. But he never sought to appeal to the mere emotions of his audiences. He never begged, but demanded. Nor did he believe in too much discussion of things that in themselves seemed so plain and axiomatic. His main concern was the work that had to be done, the results that had to be achieved. With him Zionism was a must, a self-evident thing, the only means to insure the survival of his people. Palestine must again become "Eretz Yisroel", the land of Israel, and this can be attained only through the efforts of the Jews themselves.

I recall the first speech I heard him deliver. It was in the spring of 1920, at a large gathering in the Metropolitan Opera House in New York. On the rostrum as speakers were some of the most prominent Jewish leaders of the day, Louis Marshall, Albert Einstein—then on his first trip to America —Chaim Weizmann,—and Ussishkin. He was the very last to speak, and the only one to use Hebrew as his vehicle. But it was not just a speech; it sounded more like a proclamation by a commanding general. He used short and plain-speaking words, and his sentences were short, too. Such and such is the situation, and thus and thus is the programme to be carried out. By its inordinateness, its daring, the speech made a profound impression. On the platform stood a novel type of Jew, a physically and morally powerful type. He symbolised the new Jew many of us believed would emerge as a result of the new Jewish life that was being created in the hills and valleys of Palestine. Let me also add that Ussishkin himself resembled but little the accepted Jewish type; he looked more like a Slav. Tall and powerfully built, his strong facial delineations lacked the softness we usually find in Jewish faces. Had he been attired in a military uniform with epaulets he could easily have been taken for a

Russian colonel or general giving orders to his troops on the battlefield.

It was that same year, 1920, that I first became acquainted with him. It was Ussishkin's first visit to the United States. I came to know him better in subsequent years, more especially in 1925 when I visited him on a Friday night at his home in Jerusalem. I shall have more to say presently about that to me memorable visit. I also met him at several of the Zionist congresses and again at a Zionist conference in Washington. Each time I found added cause for admiring the unusual energy and will-power of this man who remained so strong, in mind as in body, even when veering towards old age. It was plain that Zionism was his only life-content to which he devoted all of his powers. It was his only occupation, and the only thing that mattered to him. As such he served to me and others as a symbol of what is expected of every one calling himself Zionist.

I write this as the question of Palestine's future is being weighed in the balance by the United Nations, and from all indications we are nearing a solution to the age-old dream of countless millions of Jews, their restoration to nationhood in their ancient land. In that realization history will not overlook the work of Menahem Mendel Ussishkin and his trusted followers whose ceaseless efforts in redeeming the soil of Palestine and its cultivation by tens of thousands of colonists, gave the Jews their strongest argument, the fact that they have actually taken possession of the land and made it their own by their labor, sweat and blood. It was this one fact, which could not be denied or ignored, that lent as strong an impetus as anything else in the decision reached by the special commission on Palestine of the United Nations to recommend to partition off the land between the Jews and the Arabs. The rise of the Jewish State is as much the work of Ussishkin as of any of the other leaders who have guided the destinies of Zionism from its very inception.

Ussishkin played a most important part in bringing the claim of the Jewish people to Palestine before the Versailles Peace Conference at the close of the First World War. England had already issued the Balfour Declaration (1917) but the victorious nations sitting in judgment on defeated Germany, Austria and Turkey had to ratify the British policy in Palestine. Ussishkin was one of the large sized Jewish delegation that appeared before that memorable international gathering. When his turn came to speak, he chose Hebrew for his medium. He knew quite well that neither Clemenceau nor Woodrow Wilson, Lloyd George or Orlando of Italy would understand a single word of what he said (he, of course, made sure that his argument would reach them in translation), yet he did it as a demonstration of the fact that he was speaking for a people that was far from dead, a people that had preserved its soul throughout the nineteen hundred years of its suspended national life and still had its Hebrew language, now greatly enriched by the work of the Jewish sages and scholars of the many centuries.

True to himself was Ussishkin also in his stand on Arab-Jewish relations in Palestine. He remained adamant against any and every suggestion of a compromise in this question. Eretz Yisroel must be what its name indicates, the land which belongs to Israel historically and which Jews must reconquer by their own economic and spiritual labors. Hence he was most outspoken against the "Brith Shalom" (peace covenant) group headed by Judah L. Magnes which sought to solve the problem through the establishment of a bi-national State. When Dr. Magnes one year opened the new school season at

the Hebrew University with an address in which he advocated such a scheme, he was immediately answered and assailed by Ussishkin who was in the audience. The one solution he saw was the purchase of more and more land for
cultivation by the Jews. To this end he organised the Jewish
National Fund ("Keren Kayemeth L'Yisroel") and himself
travelled in the United States and other parts of the world to
raise funds. Many millions of dollars were thus collected
through his efforts.

Yet even this remarkable man, with the iron will and
dictatorial firmness so rare among Jews—was at the core of
his being only a Jew, with all the softness and tenderness
usually characteristic of our people. There were moments
when he revealed himself in a new light, as one capable of
much and great friendliness. It was then that he showed his
true self. The other side of the coin, his rigid intransigeance
in all that pertained to Jewish nationalism as he saw it, was
in reality a mere facade, a mask necessary under the prevailing circumstances.

As already stated, I had occasion to see Ussishkin at his
Jerusalem home on a Friday evening when I spent two hours
with him in a very friendly Sabbath-Eve atmosphere. On
my return to America late that summer (1925) I published
an article about that experience in the New York "Hadoar",
which is proof of how deeply impressed I was with that
visit, the memory of which is still as fresh in my mind as
though it had occurred only yesterday.

I recall that on my way to keep the appointment I was
somewhat ill at ease. I had never before met him socially—
our previous meetings were at congresses or conferences
which permitted nothing more intimate than a handshake
and an exchange of a few words. I had heard that he was
severe and unbending in his demands from people, intoler-

ant in many things, among them in his aversion to the use of Yiddish which he despised as a jargon picked up by the Jews in their wanderings. While yet in Russia he was said to have said that Jews there should speak either Russian or Hebrew, Yiddish being deemed unfit for use in polite society. Bearing this in mind I decided to be on my guard that evening as I was meandering through the pitch-dark streets of the Jerusalem of that time, led by my good friends Mr. and Mrs. Zalman Kotliar. It was they who had arranged the visit for me, and without their kind guidance I should have had a difficult time in finding the apartment.

It therefore came as a most happy surprise when face to face with this "terrible" man, that instead of the ogre I had pictured him to be I beheld a truly human man. There was nothing of the dictator and no trace of the fanatic in the Menahem Mendel Ussishkin who sat opposite me that evening. He laughed merrily, told many humorous stories— and all in Yiddish, a rich, juicy, Lithuanian Yiddish, mixed with many Hebrew, Russian and English words, and he did it naturally and spontaneously and not because I gave him the least cause for it. I should add that even the thoughts he expressed that evening, when he discussed the more serious aspects of the Zionist situation of that time, were moderately put, with due appreciation of the thinking processes of his antagonists and of the causes that led to the position they took.

We are seated in a large brilliantly-lit room at a white-covered table drinking Russian tea and eating fruits and cookies which handsome and festively-arrayed Madame Ussishkin keeps serving us with. Besides the Kotliars and myself there is also the eminent Hebrew novelist, Samuel E. Agnon, and Ussishkin keeps up his barrage of stories and anecdotes, and all in Yiddish. Was it because he thought he might make me feel more at home in his presence by not forcing me to converse in unaccustomed Hebrew, seeing that he himself was not full master of the English? That was the impression I carried away with me, and because of which he endeared himself to me. I left him in a much happier frame of mind than when I crossed his threshold. It was a little thing which showed him up as the great man that he was.

Shmaryahu Levin

ONE VERY COLD, snowy Sunday in 1915 I met Dr. Shmaryahu Levin at the Grand Central Station in New York, to carry out a joint mission in behalf of the Zionist Organization of America. We were to address two large gatherings in Connecticut, in New Haven, where we spoke that afternoon, and in Hartford where we appeared in the evening. I was the English speaker for the benefit of those who did not understand Yiddish, the language used by Dr. Levin. But the overwhelming majority of our audiences had no need of an English speech. They flocked there by their hundreds and thousands to hear one of the most gifted of Yiddish orators—it was he who was the main attraction. Levin was not only a talented speaker, he also had the advantage of knowing the psychology of the people he was addressing. He played on their soul-strings, appealed to their emotions, and told them tales from the Midrash and Aggadah which so many of them, in those far off days, still remembered and appreciated from their own *Cheder* days.

It was not the first time I had met him. Our acquaintance dated back to 1906, when Dr. Levin made his initial visit to the United States. I then had occasion to note his many-sided gifts as a cultured personality. But it was on that Connecticut trip that I came in close contact with him, in the few hours we were together on the train and in the hotel at Hartford, where we remained over night. After the meeting in that city we spent hours together discussing the problems of the Jewish people. It was the beginning of a friendship which lasted through the years.

Shmaryahu Levin was first and foremost a Jewish nationalist, and he occupied himself with Zionism to the exclusion of everything else. He had no other vocation, and nothing else mattered much to him. Even when he delved into literary work, or promoted the business side of the *Dvir* publishing house, in which he was a partner with Bialik, it was only as a means of fostering and strengthening the Jewish nationalist movement. He wielded a powerful pen both in Hebrew, in which he began his activity as a writer, and in Yiddish, in which he wrote most of his books. His writings had but one aim—to clarify and to popularize Zionism among the Jewish masses. Because of his Zionism he suffered not a little. Easily angered in a controversy, he now and then found himself in troublous situations. He also was compelled to be a wanderer most of his life, travelling across half the world to bring to his widely scattered brethren the Zionist gospel. But all the hardships he encountered he accepted smilingly and cheerfully, a price he willingly paid for his life's ideal.

Levin was a Jewish celebrity long before his debut in America in 1906. His fame had preceded him here as a noted preacher and even more as one of the few deputies elected by the six million Jews of Russia to represent them in the Imperial Duma, the parliament which the Czar found himself compelled to grant to his subjects, after the Russian debacle in the war with Japan and the unrest and uprisings of the Russian masses which followed. A liberal though not a reformer in religion, Dr. Levin was never happier than when serving his Jewish people.

His was a courageous struggle against tremendous odds in the milieu of bigotry and political anarchy in which he and other Russian-Jewish leaders were fated to labor. Born in Swislowicz, a small town in White Russia, of well-to-do parents who, though religious-minded were not fanatical, he received the traditional *Cheder* schooling in his childhood, but instead of going to some Yeshiva when old enough, he was sent to high school at Minsk. As a youth he was drawn into the Haskalah movement and was greatly influenced by Peretz Smolenskin and his *Hashachar* articles. He received his academic education in Germany, first in Berlin University and later at the University of Koenigsberg, where he obtained his Ph.D. degree. Already noted for his Hebrew artices in *Hamaggid* and *Haschiloah*, he returned to Russia where, after his marriage, he settled down as a worker in the Hebrew publishing house of *Ahiasaf* in Warsaw. A few years later he was elected as "Government Rabbi" (a sort of official representative of the Jewish community before the Government authorities) first in Grodno and later in Yekaterinoslav. Unhappy in this position, which he found irksome and offensive to his dignity as a Jew, he was happy when called to Wilna to become the preacher and spiritual leader of the liberal synagague of the city. There he enjoyed several years of satisfying activity as a teacher, preacher and leader in many a worthy cause, more especially in *Hibbat Tzion* which was to be transformed into the Zionist movement after Theodore Herzl appeared upon the scene. From Wilna he went to St. Petersburg as a member of the Duma where he experienced a stormy existence and became a marked man for the reactionary forces and the Black Hundreds which the Czarist regime had called into being.

When Czar Nicholas prorogued the Duma, Shmaryahu Levin was among the deputies who went to Viborg, Finland, right across the frontier, there to sign the famous "Manifesto" in which they called upon the Russian people to fight for their political freedom and to refuse paying taxes and giving their sons to the army until their rights were established. For this bold challenge to the autocratic regime, the deputies were exposed to severe penalties. The Jewish deputies in particular were faced with grave reprisals. One of them, Herzenstein, who was staying in the same summer place with Levin in Finland, was found murdered. Levin knew that he, too, could expect the worst, and when informed that he was being shadowed by suspicious-looking characters, he escaped to St. Petersburg and went into hiding. Luck was with him; a high Government official whom he managed to interview obtained a passport for him. He made his way across the frontier and into Germany. His career in his native Russia was at an end. A much richer career awaited him in the United States and in Palestine.

These are but a few headlines of a rich and colorful life, as Levin describes it in his four-volume autobiography. The book is one of the classics in modern Jewish literature. Three of the volumes were prepared during his stay in the United States, in Yiddish, and were subsequently translated into Hebrew, English and German. The fourth volume, originally in Hebrew, was written in Palestine and published in Tel-Aviv, and is of special importance to us because most of it is devoted to the account of his escape from Russia and his arrival in New York in 1906. He testifies that though he wrote mostly in Yiddish in order to reach the largest number of readers, Hebrew remained his one and only love. Even when he wrote in other languages, he states, he would first think his argument through in Hebrew.

But far more than a writer, Shmaryahu Levin was a speaker, and it was as such that he impressed himself on the Jewish people. As a writer he had to labor and sweat, choosing and pruning his words and sentences. But on the speakers' rostrum he felt completely at ease, and he was never happier than when facing a large audience to whose minds he could appeal and in whose hearts he could plant the seed

of his ideals. Though he spoke in Yiddish, and most frequently in Orthodox synagogues, he was not a *Maggid* (old-
time Yiddish preacher), and was not even a mere moralist,
notwithstanding that the material he used for his harangues
came from the same old rabbinic sources, the Talmud, Midrash and Aggadah, to which rabbinical preachers usually
resort. He was chiefly an enlightener and clarifier who
made use of Jewish traditions and sagas, Midrashic tales
and Aggadic parables to reach the hearts of his listeners.
And he did it with marvellous ease and felicity. I do not
think that he ever "prepared" a speech. He always knew
what he was going to say; the *how* came of itself. When already on the platform his address began to assume shape
and form, aided by his rich vocabulary. He then was a cap-
tive of his own oratorical powers. The presence of a large
audience inspired him, even as the same audience was carried along with him by the pathos of his arguments. I believe it was the first time in the history of Yiddish preaching
that the speaker should be so high class, logical, convincing
and appealing, as was the case of Shmaryahu Levin.

But we should bear in mind that this talent to sway audiences was in large measure developed by the Zionist ideology which lent wings to his words as to his ideas; also that
it revealed itself in its fullest strength only after he left
Russia for the freer atmosphere of Europe and more especially of the United States. In Russia he had but little opportunity to use his gift of speech, not only because the
police had an eye on him but because the entire atmosphere
of the autocratic state was such as to cramp and hold down
a man of spirit; it either discouraged him in his efforts to
reach the people, or else drove him in the revolutionary
underground. As a "Government Rabbi" in Grodno and Yekaterinoslav Levin was especially handicapped, for he had

to report his activities to the authorities and carry out their orders. In Wilna under the cloak of a religious leader he was able to go on with his preachment somewhat more freely. As a deputy in the Duma he delivered some very powerful addresses depicting the sorry state of his people under the restrictions of the existing anti-Jewish laws, but those addresses were in Russian. Shmaryahu Levin found himself as a fully matured public speaker only after he was on the other side of the frontier where large audiences everywhere were eagerly awaiting his stirring Yiddish messages.

He describes in his memoirs the difficulties he was faced with and the humiliation he felt himself subjected to while functioning as Government Rabbi. He frequently had to appear on festive Russian occasions to represent the Jews and had to speak when he would much rather have kept silent. He writes there: "It is hard to suppress your words when the speech trembles in your heart and on your tongue. But there is no greater pain than to have to speak at a time and place when you would much prefer to keep quiet. The Government Rabbi had to deliver speeches in the synagogue seven times a year, on the birthdays of the Czar, the Czarina, the Czarewich, the Crowning anniversary, the Name Day, etc. When I accepted the position in Grodno I discovered that in addition to the customary "Hanossen Teshuah" prayer for the health and prosperity of the Czar they also were made to sing the national anthem in which thanks are offered for the autocratic and *Christian* (*"Pravoslavniy"*) Emperor, and this in the presence of the leaders of the Jewish community and of the Jewish youth. The Jewish community thus had to slap itself in the face. To be sure, everybody knew that this was but one more falsehood in the entire fraudulent system of the Czarist regime. But it was something very painful to swallow" . . .

In the United States Shruaryahu Levin, as stated, found a ready audience of hundreds of thousands of listeners, and in his day he was the foremost Zionist propagandist in the Western Hemisphere. It was due to his efforts that the Zionist movement in America had developed such strength and was able to make such a notable contribution towards the up-building of Jewish Palestine politically as well as economically.

Highly interesting is the fact, as he relates, that the very first opportunity to come to America, was afforded him by prominent non-Zionists and even anti-Zionists—the very group of whom he was so unsparing whenever he had occasion to assail their stand on the Zionist question. Immediately responsible for this visit, in 1906, was Dr. Judah L. Magnes, who by that time had become the outstanding rabbinical figure in New York and was the secretary of the Federation of American Zionists. It was Magnes who interested men like Jacob H. Schiff to extend the invitation to Dr. Levin and to finance his trip, the purpose being to have him deliver a series of addresses in New York and other cities on the Jewish situation in Russia which was then the burning question of the day. Levin fully lived up to the terms of the invitation. His first address in each place he visited was on that topic, and it was in German, and he invariably made a deep impression on the more Americanised Jews of German extraction. But after that he felt free to accept other invitations to speak before the more humble immigrant masses and to bring them the Zionist message. It is not unlikely that he felt more at home with the latter than the former.

He gives a graphic description of his very first New York meeting which was presided over by Mr. Schiff, then the "uncrowned king" of American Jewry. It took place in a huge riding academy on Madison Square, and some 10,000 crowded into the place, with another estimated 10,000 crowded out. It was at that meeting that Schiff announced that because of the persecutions of the Jews in Russia he and other Jewish bankers would do their utmost to prevent the Czar's government from obtaining a loan in the United States. This statement was flashed across the country and all over the world and furnished the big headlines in the next morning's newspapers.

In that fourth volume Levin describes the physical appearance of New York of more than 40 years ago, which he compared with other great cities of the world he had lived in. New York was to him the noisiest as well as the most wasteful of large cities. The streets at night, he wrote, were unnecessarily illumined during hours when people sleep and do not need light. He found fault also with the system of streets being called by numbers instead of names, as that deprived them of any character of their own. Nor was he happy about the artificial division of the city into "Up Town" and "Down Town". He saw in it an invidious stressing of the social differences between the rich who live in the upper part of the city and the impoverished denizens of the lower part. The gigantic New York "Ghetto" of those days amazed him, especially the circumstance that it was a purely voluntary affair and not a compulsory arrangement as in the case of many a European Jewry. He saw in this the collective will of a people that persists in its determination to survive as a racial entity and not go under through dispersion. From this point of view he assailed the efforts that were made at that time to liquidate the large ghettos through removal of Jews to the interior and smaller cities of the country. The rich Jews, he believed, were ashamed of the ghetto as a stigma on their dignity and self-respect as Jews and Americans. Were they to consult the ghetto Jews themselves, he claimed, they would discover that the latter felt quite happy and secure there.

All Jews of the East Side in those days spoke Yiddish, but there were different Yiddish dialects and pronunciations, depending upon whether one came from Lithuania or Galicia, Hungary, Roumania or Poland. These different categories of Jews had their separate sections in the huge East Side. If they were not all distinguishable during the day, since so many of the men wore beards, at night one could safely tell what section of the ghetto he was in. The test was simple: the cooking. By the smell of the dishes which the housewives specialised in, one could determine whether he was in the Galician, Roumanian or Lithuanian quarter . . .

Of his journey through the States that year he tells of his trip to Washington where he, with a delegation of prominent Jews who accompanied him, was received by President Theodore Roosevelt. In Philadelphia he met and saw much of Judge Meyer Sulzberger, whom he describes very sympathetically. Sulzberger, as well as Louis Marshall, he states, were the two prominent American Jews of German origin who gave themselves to a study of Yiddish and to reading Yiddish newspapers in order the better to fathom the soul of the immigrant Jew . . . . In Baltimore he met Henrietta Szold for the first time and tells of the admiration he felt for that gifted daughter of Israel. In Boston, where he was accompanied by Jacob de Haas, he was surprised to find William James, the eminent philosopher, in his audience every time he spoke. When he inquired of him whether he could get anything out of an address delivered in an unknown tongue, James told him that while he could not follow everything he said, he could yet grasp the drift of his thoughts. In Chicago he became intimately acquainted with Julius Rosenwald, Judge Julian Mack, and Adolf Kraus,

President of B'nai B'rith, who was very solicitous for his comfort. Dr. Emil G. Hirsch attended a meeting where Levin spoke and evidently in his honor tried to give a talk in Hebrew, but failed in the effort . . . . From there he went to Cincinnati, where he was invited by President Kaufman Kohler to address the students at the Hebrew Union College, Dr. Kohler assuring him that he had the fullest freedom to discuss Zionism, if he cared to, and Levin made good use of his opportunity. When he finished talking, however, Dr. Kohler, replied to his arguments and a controversy developed, but they parted as friends.

Having discovered America and the new Jewish life that had struck such deep roots here, Shmaryahu Levin made frequent trips to this continent, dividing his time between here and Palestine, where he established his permanent home. When World War I broke out in the summer of 1914, Levin was a traveler from the United States to Europe on a German boat. For fear of being captured by the British it returned to American territorial waters, and the passengers were disembarked at a port in Maine. Levin remained in the United States during all the war years, and kept himself occupied with writing for the Yiddish press and carrying on his Zionist activities.

That war of necessity put a stop to all Zionist work in Europe, and there was danger that the movement would be altogether atrophied. Dr. Levin, as a member of the Zionist Actions Committee, decided to do something about it. His formula was simple: American Jewry, now grown big and strong numerically and economically, must take over the work for the duration of the war. I recall the meeting which he called for that purpose in the late fall of 1914 at the Hotel Marseille, New York, to which I was invited. There were present a large number of prominent American Jewish leaders, and they organised the Provisional Zionist Congress, to function in the place of the World Zionist Congress. Among those who came to the meeting was Louis D. Brandeis, who thus made his debut as a Zionist. After that Brandeis was frequently to be seen and heard at Zionist conferences until he was named to the United States Supreme Court by President Wilson. In Baltimore in 1916, at such a conference which I attended, Brandeis and Shmaryahu Levin were the leading speakers. A year later, when America had entered the war against Germany, the Balfour Declaration was in the process of being born, and President Wilson had much to do with its formulation, for he was consulted about it by Prime Minister Lloyd George. Behind the scenes, it was Brandeis who influenced Woodrow Wilson in his approval of the exact wording of that famous document. But indirectly Shmaryahu Levin had a hand in it, for it was he, together with Jacob de Haas, who had tutored Brandeis in Zionism.

Extremely fond of the United States, where he saw the rise of a great and powerful Jewish community, Shmaryahu Levin was particularly attached to New York, where he spent most of his time in the States. Here he kept busy as a writer and speaker, and here he moved among congenial circles where he was lionised by all sections of the Jewry now grown to gigantic proportions. After his addresses on many a night, the evening would first begin for him at some well-known restaurant where he would be accompanied by many of his admiring friends and followers. In his memoirs he confesses that he would often spend the better part of the night in this fashion. He did not relish going to bed. Life for him meant staying awake. . .

[81]

Vladimir Jabotinsky

IT WAS MY GOOD FORTUNE to meet Vladimir Jabotinsky on many occasions, here in America, in Paris, where he lived, and at Zionist congresses. I saw him at work as the leader of the Revisionist Party. I read his writings and heard many of his speeches—at mass meetings where he fumed and stormed against Great Britain for her injustice to the Jews in Palestine, and against the Zionist leadership which did so little to convince the British Government of its error and to cause it to mend its ways. I also heard him at small gatherings and parlor meetings when he would curb his temper and speak in a conversational tone about the work to be done and the methods to be pursued. Dynamic, inordinately talented both as a writer and speaker, and a man of the utmost probity, Jabotinsky was a power to be reckoned with in Jewish life, whether one agreed with him or not. He simply could not be ignored. He was a strongly moral personality who won his place as Jewish leader by repeated examples of daring and heroism. The basis of his influence lay chiefly in his moral integrity, in his firm convictions because of which he more than once suffered imprisonment in Czarist Russia and in "liberated" Palestine. All in all this man with the peculiar Russian surname "Vladimir" was a great personality in whom was mirrored the tragedy as well as the greatness of the age in which he lived.

In appearance Jabotinsky was anything but attractive. Small of stature, of dark complexion, his facial features, too, were homely. He depicts himself in his autobiography as he looked in his early twenties: "boyish, and dressed like a

[83]

gypsy or bohemian". It was due to his ungainly appearance that he was once thrown out of the Odessa Municipal Theatre by the Chief of Gendarmes. Jabotinsky was already a famous journalist at that time, and as a dramatic critic for the press he had the right to come to the theatre at any time and take a seat among the notables in the front row. The Chief failed to recognise him, accused him of sneaking in where he had no right to be, and ordered him out. Greatly offended, Jabotinsky assailed the police head in vehement language—an unusual bit of daring in autocratic Russia in those early years of the century. A scandal broke loose, as a result of which Jabotinsky had to flee the city to escape the retribution that was sure to overtake him. This was but one of many similar episodes he experienced in consequence of his unprepossessing looks, as he describes them in his highly interesting memoirs.

One could easily compare Jabotinsky with other eminent Zionist leaders—with Nahum Sokolow, for instance, who was also a "wonder-child" and, like Jabotinsky, distinguished himself by his knowledge of many languages in which he both wrote and spoke. Only that Sokolow was also an eminent Jewish scholar and a Talmudist of note, which Vladimir Jabotinsky was not. He could also be compared favorably with Herzl, Nordau and Zangwill who were famous alike for their oratory as for their literary talents. Yet in many respects Jabotinsky stood in a class by himself. He was never elastic in his views and never yielding in the position he took. Even when inclined to carry out the wishes and instructions of those whom he represented, he would, in the last moment, act as he personally felt and thought on the subject. His "Revisionism" may be said to have begun from the very time he joined the Zionist ranks, though it took many years before his ideas became crystallised so that there ensued the split in Zionism. A man of his calibre could not long remain fenced in by party platforms or political maneuvers which are not always honest. As a diplomat Jabotinsky was a failure, but only because he was too decent to say amen against his real convictions. Revisionism was a development of his conception of post-Herzlian Zionism. It was Jabotinsky's way to himself, and a search of a way out of the maze of the Jewish problem which troubled him constantly and was the driving force behind all his actions.

He began like other Zionist tribunes of his day who came to the movement from the assimilationist Jewish camp after the ever-growing Antisemitism in Europe had driven them to make the necessary revision of their position as Jews. Essentially Zionism is a revolt against the abnormality of Jewish life in many lands. But it did not take Jabotinsky as long as it did Herzl or Nordau to make the necessary deductions and to arrive at the logical conclusions. He was very young when first drawn into the Zionist circle of his native city of Odessa; when he attended his first Zionist Congress in 1903 he was not quite 23. He went there as an outsider, a student and observer of the movement. He soon found himself at home there and it was as an outsider that he became the fearless critic of the flaws and weaknesses which he found in Zionist leadership. Zionism came to mean everything in the world to him, yet he did not hesitate to attack it for its own good, as he honestly believed.

He tells of his up-bringing and of the spiritual crisis he experienced before coming to Zionism, in his highly absorbing autobiography which appeared in Tel-Aviv in 1936 as a preface to the first volume of his collected Hebrew writings. It is a great pity that these memoirs do not go beyond 1914, when he was only 34 years of age, though a few additional chapters have appeared since in a Yiddish daily in

New York. As we know, his greatest achievements, which made him a national and a world Jewish figure came after that year which brought the First World War. It was in that war that he distinguished himself as the founder of the Jewish Legion which fought under British command in the Gallipoli campaign for the liberation of Palestine; it was also in the latter years that he became the leader of the Revisionist wing. But we should be grateful for the little he did give us in those pages which tell the story of his childhood and young manhood. It is a tale replete with exciting events in his own life as in that of others, in which are mixed many amusing anecdotes told in a playful and prankish manner. The book is worth reading if only for its literary value. His Hebrew, too, is unusually good. This man, who so distinguished himself as a stylist in Russian that he came to be regarded as one of the foremost Russian writers of his day, and who also wrote an excellent German and Italian, not to mention Yiddish, also acquired a unique and fascinating Hebrew style.

Born of educated and liberal-minded parents, Jabotinsky lost his father when he was but six years old, and until his sister became old enough to help earn some money, the family suffered poverty and want. He tells how, immediately after his father's death, the relatives met for a consultation on how best to help, especially as regards the future of the two children. One of them, himself a successful lawyer, expressed himself thus: "We have enough educated people in the family. Let the girl learn to be a seamstress and the boy be apprenticed to a carpenter." His mother, however, would not hear of it. She worked hard and sent the children to school. He writes adoringly of his mother's moral and spiritual qualities. A scion of a prominent and well-to-do family, and reared in great luxury, she showed marvellous

[86]

courage when, as a widow, she had to support her two children. She would often go hungry herself but never failed to bring home fresh rolls for the youngsters.

Their home in Odessa was strongly russified. Though he and his sister understood Yiddish, they never had occasion to use it, Russian being the only language employed in the house. Vladimir received his introduction to Hebrew "accidentally" when Y. H. Ravnitzky, who later became a leading Hebrew essayist and a co-worker with Chaim Nachman Bialik in the "Dvir" publishing house, took a fancy to the poor lad and volunteered to instruct him in the old tongue. Several others, students of the university mostly, offered to teach him English and French. His polyglot education thus began very early in life. But when he entered the "Gymnasium" (High School) he turned out to be a very poor student, and more than once he was sent home in disgrace —not, he assures us, because of Antisemitism, which did not yet exist in the Odessa educational circles of those days, but because of his conduct. He would not submit to the requirements and disciplines of the institution, and if he ever studied it was not what was prescribed but what he chose. He left the Gymnasium without getting his diploma. In like manner, in later years, when about to graduate from the university, he left without a diploma. In a certain sense he was a fatalist, resigned to having circumstances dictate his actions. The little Russian word *tahk* (So!) played an important part in his life. He can find no explanation why he acts thus and not otherwise, not even as the logic of a given situation would require. He can only say: *Tahk!*

In many ways Vladimir took after his father. The elder Jabotinsky was held in high esteem by his neighbors, and was noted for his mentality and good-heartedness. He held an important post as administrator of a Russian Steamship company. His name was Jonah, in Russian "Yevghenni" (Eugene). One day the head of the company, in a spirit of admiration, said to him: "Yevghenni, you are a *ghenni* (genius)." Noted for his kindness, he had a good word for everybody. Once, when informed that an employee was stealing from him, he replied: "He who steals from me is poorer than I—and maybe he had a right to what he took". Vladimir Jabotinsky then remarks that this streak of character, good-naturedness and shiftlessness, are among the weaknesses he inherited from his father . . . .

He began his literary work quite early in his youth, and this, too, had some connection with his failure as a student. He neglected his school work in order to give himself to writing. His first steps in literature were translations into Russian of parts of Canticles and of poems by Jehuda Leib Gordon, and also of Poe's "The Raven". The newspapers to whom he kept sending these literary efforts rejected them unceremoniously.

Shortly thereafter he was introduced to the editor of the daily *Odesski Listok*, to whom he showed his translation of Edgar Allen Poe. The editor recognised his promising talents. He offered to send him to Berne, Switzerland, as correspondent of the paper and also to enable him to enter the University. Vladimir accepted the offer, though it meant giving up the Gymnasium where he had another 18 months to go. Of this episode he wrote: "The young reader of our day will find it hard to understand what a Gymnasium education meant for a Jew forty years ago. It meant a diploma, the right to enter a (Russian) university, the right to live outside the 'Pale'—in short a human instead of a dog's life. And here I am already in the 7th class and in another year and a half will be entitled to don the blue cap and the black uniform of a university student. What madness is this to throw it all away and ruin all my prospects, and why?" He found no answer to the query, except the above-mentioned *tahk*.

But when we look at his life's work and the many aspirations which filled and guided him, we find that that little monosyllabic *tahk* was what forged his destiny and made possible his training as a Jewish leader. It was necessary that Jabotinsky should tear himself away from Russia for a few years, and on his way to Berne pass through the thickly populated Jewish communities of Galicia and Hungary, where for the first time he witnessed the full degradation of ghetto poverty and misery and thus got an inkling of what the Jewish problem was like. In his russified life in Odessa he never saw anything like it, and it impressed him painfully and repellingly. In Berne he is drawn into the local "Russian" student colony which consisted almost entirely of Jewish emigres. There he also came in contact with Russian revolutionaries such as Lenin and Plekhanov, and with Jewish nationalists like Nachman Syrkin and Chaim Zhitlovsky. He attended lectures at the university and sent articles and news-letters to his paper under the pseudonym of "Altalina", and these quickly established his reputation as a correspondent and commentator on world affairs. In the student colony he heard the young people debate Socialism and also Zionism, and himself took part in the discussions.

He remained in Berne but a short time. His natural restlessness drove him on to Rome where he entered the university and continued his newspaper work. The few years he stayed in Italy were the most important of his life. There he quenched his thirst for knowledge in subjects that were of special interest to him, like history, sociology and philology, and two of the Italian professors exerted a special influence upon him. But, as already stated, he left the university just as he was about to graduate and returned to Russia where the noted daily *Odesskiya Novosti* offered him a high post at a lucrative salary. On his way home he again passed through Galicia and Hungary and now, he wrote, there awakened in him his Jewish national consciousness.

In Odessa important social and literary activities awaited him—and also police raids at his home and imprisonment in the Odessa jail for seven weeks. In addition to feuilletons and book reviews he also wrote dramas, which were produced on the stage of the Municipal Theater, but as a dramatist he was not much of a success. Curiously, one of his leading dramatic efforts, called "Blood", was a decidedly pacifistic play. He who later organised the Jewish Legion and fought in World War I so gallantly, and who at the beginning of World War II agitated so forcefully for a Jewish Army, in that play condemned war from every viewpoint, no matter what the causes or provocations. But this was only a passing phase of his mental evolution, for shortly after the play was staged the Kishineff massacre took place, followed by other bloody pogroms against Jews in many cities. This led to the formation of Jewish self-defense groups and Jabotinsky became the leader of the movement in Odessa.

The episode with the Chief of Gendarmes, which compelled him to flee from Odessa, had other important consequences for him. He arrived in St. Petersburg, where his reputation as a journalist opened all the newspaper doors to him. A new daily newspaper by the name of *Russ* was about to be started and its founder was Alexei Souvorin, a son of the arch-Antisemite of Russian journalism, Souvorin of the ill-famed *Novoye Vremiya*. But the son was not a follower of his father; the newspaper he established was a clean journal. Jabotinsky was at once engaged at what was then considered a good salary in Russia, 200 roubles a month for two weekly articles. But his work on *Russ* was only a side-issue with him. His chief work in the Russian capital was for a Russo-Jewish monthly, the *Yevreiskaya Zhisn* (Jewish Life) which he established with the help of several comrades. It was a Zionist journal which, of course, subsequently became an organ of Revisionism when Jabotinsky organised that movement. On all of his wanderings after he was forced to leave Russia, Jabotinsky took this journal with him, publishing it first in Berlin and later in Paris, where it appeared until the outbreak of the Second World War.

Jabotinsky had his own philosophy on Zionism, a philosophy which helps explain his Revisionism. Himself a foe of everything that oppressed and enslaved, he nursed a tendency towards that absolute individual freedom which wellnigh borders on anarchism. His main concern was not the well-being of society as a whole, but of the individual in it. He explained his thesis by paraphrasing the first verse in the book of Genesis thus: "In the beginning God created the individual". Every individual is a God-created being and a king in his own right, enjoying an absolutely equal standing with every other individual. It is better that the individual transgress against society than that society transgress against the individual, because society is made for the individual and not the other way around. At the same time he assures us that this thesis in no way is a refutation of the nationalistic ideal, for a nation, too, is an individual in the collective, and it is not wrong to say: "In the beginning God created the nation". Nations, too, are entitled to their place in the sun, their freedom of struggle for survival and prosperity. Free will is the dominating requirement for the individual, and when one assumes the yoke of service to his particular nation, he is within his right so long as he does it not from outward compulsion but from choice.

It was this basic life-philosophy of his which determined his course as a Zionist. When he attended his first Zionist congress in Basel, in 1903, he wandered around among the delegates who hardly took notice of the strange-looking boy. He knew nothing of the Zionist organization and of the problems before the Congress. "I was introduced", he writes, "to a tall and slim young man with a black goatee and a shiny bald head. His name was Dr. Weizmann, and I had been told that he was the head of the 'opposition'.. Immediately I felt that my place, too, was in the 'opposition', though I did not know what or whom to oppose . . . Later, when I saw the same young man in a cafe, surrounded by friends and engaged in a spirited discussion, I came over and asked: 'Would I disturb you?' and Weizmann answered: 'You are disturbing', and I went away". It was Jabotinsky's first encounter with Weizmann and began the ideological conflict between the two which lasted all through Jabotinsky's life.

(In Dr. Weizmann's autobiography, "Trial and Error", the first President of Israel pays high tribute to Jabotinsky, who impressed him as the "boy wonder", when he first saw and heard him, by his oratory and his mastery of "some half-dozen languages". He also tells of Jabotinsky's seeking to find himself in the Zionist ideology, and that his way, too, was by "trial and error". Says Weizmann: "His speeches at the early Congresses were provocative in tone but left no very distinct impression, so that one did not know, for instance, whether he was for Uganda or against, whether he condoned Herzl's visit to Von Plehve, Russia's bitterly Anti-semitic Minister of the Interior, or condemned it" (page 63). But in later years Weizmann discovered the truly sterling qualities of Jabotinsky of whose efforts to found, in Alexandria, Egypt, a Jewish battalion to fight in the First World War he writes: "It is almost impossible to describe the difficulties and disappointments which Jabotinsky had to face. I know of few people who could have stood up to them, but his pertinacity, which flowed from his devotion, was simply fabulous. He was discouraged and derided on every hand. Joseph Cowen, my wife, who remained his friend until his death, and I, were almost alone in our support of him. The Zionist Executive was of course against him; the non-Zionist Jews looked on him as a sort of portent. While he was working for the Jewish Legion we invited him to stay in our London house, to the discontent of many Zionists" (p. 167). Nevertheless Jabotinsky did not hesitate to oppose and fight Weizmann on matters of principle though they remained friends and respected each other to the last. I was myself an eye-witness to Jabotinsky's vehement onslaught on Weizmann's policies at the 1931 Congress at Basel. That attack led to important consequences, for it resulted in the formation of the Revisionist party which was later to play a great role in the Jews' struggle against the British in Palestine, the formation of the "Irgun" underground, and the eventual abandonment by Great Britain of her Palestine mandate.)

His first speech at the Zionist Congress of 1903 was the cause of much annoyance and disorder among the delegates by the sheer fact of his mentioning Herzl's trip to Russia that year to intercede with Von Plehve, a subject they had all agreed upon to avoid and thus spare Dr. Herzl any possible embarrassment. Herzl at the time of Jabotinsky's speech was closeted with a few friends in a nearby room, and at the height of the commotion rushed on the platform. Turning to Weizmann, he asked what the young man was saying (Herzl did not understand Russian, the language Jabotinsky used). Weizmann replied: "Quatch!" (nonsense). Herzl then ruled Jabotinsky off the platform. Those were the first words Herzl ever addressed to him. Yet Jabotinsky remained a great admirer of the Zionist leader, and his "Revisionism" was based on the slogan: "Back to Herzl".

Jabotinsky died in America in the midst of the campaign which he came here to wage during the first year of the Second World War, in behalf of the Jewish Army idea. He wanted Jews to fight in the war as Jews, for that fact would strengthen their claim to Palestine. He foresaw the tragedy that was to befall the Jewish people in Europe at the hands of Hitler. I was present at the huge mass meeting he addressed on that subject at the Brooklyn Academy of Music in May of that year, and several months later, in August, 1940, I attended his funeral where thousands of people gathered to do honor to their fallen leader. To the last he was a heroic fighter for his people's dignity, honor and safety, and in that people's annals his name and memory will surely be enshrined.

Chaim Nachman Bialik

IN MY DAY I have exchanged letters with many of the leading Hebrew writers of the age. Chaim Nachman Bialik was one of the few with whom I have never corresponded—I had no occasion for it. Of the 1500 letters contained in the five volumes of Bialik's correspondence, published in Tel Aviv some twenty years ago, there is included but one small letter of his to me, and it was not in answer to one I wrote him. It was merely an acknowledgment of a book I had sent him in 1928.

Instead, I had numerous occasions to meet this great master of the Hebrew word and Hebrew poetry. I met him in different parts of the globe—here in the United States; at his home in Tel Aviv; in Berlin, where I found him on a sick bed in a hospital; and finally at the Zionist Congress in Basel in 1931. Every such encounter was an experience thrilling and inspiring.

He was, beyond a question, one of the most interesting figures the Jewish world has produced. He was a truly great man, and in the sum of his greatness I include not only his astonishing literary talents and his unequaled achievements as poet, translator, editor and publisher, but also his rare human qualities as comrade, friend and loyal Jew. One has to bear all these things in mind in order to form a true estimate of Bialik. Aside from his poetic creativeness, which placed him in the forefront of our modern Hebrew culture, he achieved greatly in other lines of endeavor. He was a master of Hebrew prose no less than of verse, wrote marvellous sketches of Jewish life in Russia, composed fascinating tales for children based on Biblical themes, and translated into Hebrew Schiller's "Wilhelm Tell", Cervantes' "Don Quixote", and Shakespeare's "Julius Caesar". Together with his life-long friend and co-worker, Y. H. Ravnitzky, he issued such valuable works as "Sefer Ha-Agadah" (Book of Jewish legends) in three volumes; and edited, with commentaries, new editions of the *Mishna*. He spent many years in the study of the works of the mediaeval Hebrew poets, and published with the necessary annotations the collective poems of Solomon Ibn Gabirol. He thus made possible the preservation intact of much of our Hebraic culture which otherwise might have become lost. Yet were we to limit ourselves to the purely literary Bialik, there is danger of our overlooking much that served to make him so rare a phenomenon among the great figures our age was privileged to know.

The "Orem Bochur" (impecunious student) of the Volozhin Yeshiva who, when taking his first steps in literature, was so timid and unsure of himself and so obsessed with the sense of his own inadequacy and inferiority as to be afraid to go to see Ahad Haam when in Odessa, shortly thereafter revealed himself as the leading Hebrew bard of the centuries since the days of Yehuda Halevi and quickly became the adored master of Hebrew verse. It all sounds rather legendary now, almost two decades after his death, yet we know that even today Bialik is much of a living presence with the Hebrew reading public. His demise at the age of 61 (1934) only served to enlarge the halo about him. Those of us who were close to him are still awestruck at the riddle which he presented, as the man who combined within himself so large a measure of the abstractly spiritual and the concretely earthly, who could so gracefully mount his Pegasus to soar towards the clouds, and also descend into the depths of human pain and anguish, of teeth-gnashing and vengeance-seeking. The literary genius, the like of whom the world sees but once in a century or more, appears to us also in the guise of the affable good fellow, understanding, sympathetic, human. Like all potent spirits, Bialik wrought not for his own pleasure and satisfaction, but for his fellow-men, and not merely for his own day but for all time to come. The Bialik who wrote such immortal classics as "The Scroll of Fire", "The Desert Dead", "The Talmud Student", "The City of Slaughter", and many other masterpieces, in his every-day life remained the same plain and unassuming man of the people, the modest and humble comrade, with no trace of any conscious self-importance.

I shall yet return to the literary Bialik and to the factors and forces that made him possible. Right now I want to describe the human Bialik as I found him the few times it was my good fortune to meet him. As already stated, my first meeting with him was in New York. On a cold foggy day in February, 1926, I was one of a large group of Hebraists, Zionists, Jewish journalists and communal workers from the Metropolitan area that went to meet his boat, the Cunard Liner *Mauritania* on which he and Mrs. Bialik were passengers. It was his first and only visit to America, and he came here in the interest of the *Keren Hayesod*, or the Palestine Foundation Fund.

We got on the tug early, shortly after daybreak. Our plans were to take the Bialiks to their hotel and have the benefit of their company the better part of the day. But the plans miscarried. Red-tape on the ship retained the passengers pretty nearly the entire day. While waiting we sang Palestinian and Zionist songs and debated our perennial Jewish problems. Finally our patience was rewarded, as we beheld Bialik and his wife coming down the gangplank. A handclapping, a rush to shake his hand, a kissing with several of his friends and relatives who were in our group, and Bialik at last found himself on the soil of America. In the eyes of not a few of us tears appeared and one man, himself a noted poet, bent down and kissed his hand. In all that melee and excitement I stood on the fringe watching the not tall, stoutish man with the bald head and round, friendly face whom I saw for the first time. Somehow I could not dissociate the man from the poet as I saw him trying to make his way through the jostling, pushing crowd. I thought: So this is the author of "Ha-Brecha" (The Pond); there stands the "Methe Midbar" (The Desert Dead); there walks "Al Saf Beth Ha-Medrash" (On The Threshold of the School House). For the moment I could think only of the works which had afforded me and countless others so much joy and evoked such great admiration.

On subsequent occasions I discovered that Bialik the man contributed not a little to the popularity of Bialik the poet. What other famous Hebrew writers may have lacked—a fraternal attitude towards their fellows and a sympathetic interest in their welfare—Chaim Nachman Bialik possessed in a large measure. I believe his native friendliness exercised a beneficent influence upon his talents as as a poet. Not that the man in Bialik was greater than the poet in him; yet I am convinced that in order to be a great poet one must first be a great man, possessing those virtues of mind and heart which are the unmistakable signs of greatness. This, assuredly, Bialik was.

Strongly entrenched in my memory is his first appearance before a New York audience, a day or two after his arrival. It took place at the large auditorium of the Mecca Temple (now the City Center) on West 55th Street, in the presence of some 3000 persons, among them the elite of

New York Jewry and of other communities. On the stage sat leaders of the Zionist Organization, representatives of the Hebrew movement, of the Jewish press and Jewish cultural groups. Judge Julian Mack presided, and among those who paid him tribute were Nahum Sokolow, Shmaryahu Levin, the Yiddish poet Yehoash, and Joseph Barondess. Bialik did not begin to understand Mack's English introduction with its highly laudatory description of the "Hebrew bard", but he was so swept away by the ovation of the inflamed audience that he lost himself when he rose to speak. The shouts of "Hedad" (Hooray!), the clapping of 6,000 hands and the repeated singing of "Hatikvah" had a confounding effect on our poet. His speech in Yiddish, mixed with many Russian words, was not a success. It was not the fiery, captivating oration his American audience expected from him, though it should have known that poetry and oratory do not always go hand in hand . . . Men and women leaving the place were overheard giving vent to their disappointment and I myself went away with the feeling that he was not much of an attraction on the speaker's platform. No doubt, Bialik himself was first to sense his failure to impress his listeners that evening. But I have had other occasions to hear him speak when I saw him in a different light and had to change my estimate of his ability as a speaker. In a more homelike environment, especially when speaking in Hebrew before intellectuals and writers, Bialik proved himself capable of rising to great oratorical heights. In Palestine he was greatly sought after as a speaker. During his American tour, too, after he had become more acclimated and more cognizant of American mass psychology, his speeches were more successful.

I got a close-up of him some months after that, when I spent a few hours with Dr. Shmaryahu Levin at the latter's apartment in the Hotel Commodore. Bialik lived in the same hotel, only a few doors from Levin, and upon the latter's apprising him by telephone of my visit, he came into the room. Smiling, talkative, witty, he captivated me at once. It was during the Passover week, and Dr. Levin had ordered tea, wine and cakes which looked like Passover products, and to give it a still more festive appearance there were also a few Matzos. Bialik could not refrain from sarcasm in pointing to this sign of "religiosity" in eating Passover food served in a non-Kosher hotel. The joke was good naturedly directed also at me as a Reform rabbi. It must have been I, he said, who gave the Commodore Hotel the necessary "Hekhsher" (rabbinical permit) in keeping with the prescriptions of the Reform "Shulkhan Arukh" (manual for religious observance). But since he, too, partook of the food, the same as Levin, I found it easy to get back at him. I told him that now that he had become a "Goy" (a sinner) like the rest of us, I would propose him for honorary membership of the Central Conference of American Rabbis . . . .

About half a year later I had an opportunity to come in even closer touch with him, this time in his home in Tel-Aviv on my second visit to Palestine, in 1927. I went to see him at the very fine and spacious residence that had been built for him, with the help of admiring friends, on the street named after him, "Rechov Bialik". I had been requested by an American friend to take up with him a certain matter in connection with his publishing firm, the "Dvir", and my orders were to lay the matter before him personally. I found him at work with Ravnitzky. On seeing me he pushed aside the manuscripts he was examining, introduced me to Ravnitzky, to his parents-in-law, Mr. and Mrs. Averbach, who were living with him, and to his wife, "Manitchka", whom I had already met in New York. Then he took me up to the flat roof of his house and with great pride pointed out the progress Tel-Aviv had made in the two years since my previous visit—the new buildings that had sprung up, the additional streets that had been laid out, and the fine mansion of the City Hall, the "Iriyah", which had been constructed not far from his home. Like all Palestinian Jews, Bialik was exceedingly proud of the growth of his Tel-Aviv, the first all-Jewish city to be built by Jews and through Jewish efforts only.

I am mentioning these "little" things because all such seemingly unimportant matters are indications of the true character of a great man. Bialik was extremely affable and hospitable, and once interested in a man he would go to any length to be of help and service to him. Many of his published letters reveal this trait. Our conversation that day brought out much of the tenderness of which he was capable and by which I was greatly touched. He wanted me to know that he appreciated my taking the long trip to Palestine for the second time in two years. No Jew is worthy of the name, he said, if he fails to make periodic visits to Eretz Yisorel when in a position to do so. He also indicated his concern about my being a "lonely stranger" far away from home and family. After spending the first Friday evening at his home, he made me promise to be his guest again at the Sabbath meal the following Friday evening, if I were still in town—an invitation I was happy to accept.

Those two Friday evenings in Bialik's home are, I believe, among the most memorable of my life. I can never forget the atmosphere of ineffable Sabbath peace and serenity which dominated each of those occasions. The meal was served in the garden where the table was placed amidst a profusion of shrubs and flowers. In addition to the Sabbath candles there was the illumination from strong electric lights and, perhaps even more so, from the myriads of brilliant stars that studded the horizon. The setting was perfect. At the white-covered and food-laden table there were, in addition to the inmates, Mr. and Mrs. Averbach, Bialik, his wife and myself, also two other guests from America in the persons of Mr. and Mrs. Peretz Hirshbein. Hirshbein, the noted Yiddish poet, playwright and global traveler, was a serious-looking man who never smiled and who carried himself as if crouching, Atlas-like, under the crushing burden of a world perched upon his spare shoulders. He was of the arguing type, and he addressed Bialik with the familiar "Du" (thou) instead of the conventional "Ihr" (you) in the Yiddish conversation which the two carried on. Bialik was the very antithesis of Hirshbein. He was full of laughter, and kept entertaining his guests with stories and anecdotes and with his mimicry of people. During and after the meal other guests arrived, for it had become an established custom for neighbors and friends to visit the Bialiks on the Sabbath. Passers-by, too, were in the habit of watching from the sidewalk the scene inside the garden, straining their ears to catch some of the words that were coming from the mouth of their idolised poet.

Though unaffected by the adulation and plaudits of his people, Bialik could boast of having achieved his greatest reward, financial no less than spiritual, ever to come to a Hebrew writer and poet. He was the universally acknowledged leader of Hebrew culture for many years before his death; a whole library of books and essays about his place in literature grew up in his life time, and since his passing, notably the "Sefer Bialik" which appeared on the occasion of his sixtieth birthday, and the large-sized annuals, called "Knesseth" which are devoted to a study of his personality and his writings. More than ten such volumes have appeared,

He also received much material benefit. His books were circulated throughout the world, and the publishing business he established under the name of "Dvir", proved highly successful, and is still a going concern to this day. Since his passing the house he lived in has become a national shrine for Palestinian Jewry, has been made into a museum, and travelers from far and wide come there to look at the thousands of volumes and historic documents it houses and to breathe the air in the place where for many years lived and labored this great son of Israel.

The unusual recognition and appreciation shown to Chaim Nachman Bialik by the Jewish people was visibly demonstrated in my presence on his first Yahrzeit in July, 1935, when I again found myself in Tel-Aviv. On learning from the newspapers that there would be special exercises that evening at his late home, I went there and was an eye-witness to an unusual scene. The large house was completely filled with people, and men and women who could not find seats stood on the steps or occupied the side walks in front of the building. The lengthy programme was in charge of Asher Barasch and other literary celebrities of the city, and consisted of the reading of excerpts from his poems, essays and sketches. It was continued on the following morning when a huge throng of leaders from all over Palestine gathered at his grave, and a memorial service was carried out, with Ravnitzky chanting the "El Moleh Rachamim". On my way home from the cemetery the thought came to me that this great reverence to a Hebrew writer was in itself an indication that the Jewish nation was fast reaching maturity on Palestine's soil. None of the great Hebrew literary masters in Europe, who preceded Bialik, ever received such rewards and honors, notwithstanding that they had numerous admirers. Neither Abraham Mapu, the father of the Hebrew novel, nor Peretz Smolenskin, Judah Leib Gordon nor David Frischman, not even Ahad Haam or any others among the builders of the modern Hebrew literature knew that they had a public behind them that was duly grateful for their labors and attainments. Most of them suffered penury and privation. A great change for the better has taken place in this respect in Palestine. The Jewish people has learned to revere and reward talent and genius and thus showed that it has come of age.

Who and what was Chaim Nachman Bialik? He was a product not merely of his own age and generation. Countless Jewish generations that preceded him with their spiritual strivings, their national longings, and their code of moral living made him possible. His genius stemmed from his ancient people and his own generation, which placed its special stamp upon him, merely helped bring it to the surface because it was an epoch-making generation—a generation that stood at the cross-roads of Jewish history and was faced with the need of breaking with its past and of making itself over in the process.

The cruel fate which befell the Jews in Czarist Russia, where 6 million of them were drowning in their own blood while in nearly all other parts of the world Jews had been emancipated (at least on paper), had its effect on those hapless victims and made them restless, embittered, rebellious, the result being that their sense of frustration became even more poignant. The great outside world with its possibilities of freedom and human dignity from which they were excluded stirred and lured them and at the same time also frightened them. They wanted freedom but were afraid of the innovations it would bring them. They wondered if they could still remain Jews when politically free, for they knew that in Germany, France and other lands where Jews were enjoying such freedom (again, at least on paper), not a few of them also had become assimilated to the extent of becoming totally alienated from their noble heritage. Emigration across the Atlantic loomed as a necessary solution, but America, too, whither the emigration streamed, frightened them. The old Beth Ha-Medrash (house of study) with its stringent disciplines, still held them down. There came up the old question, Talmudic in origin, of how to "break the barrel and at the same time preserve its wine". Zionism, or *Hibbat Tzion* as it was known in pre-Herzl days, came as a compromise. It meant politically free Jews in a thoroughly Jewish milieu, emigration to Palestine where a new Jewish life is to sprout through Jewish effort, energy and enterprise. This ideal produced its preachers and its prophets. And among them Chaim Nachman Bialik, with his poetic swing, his Jewish zeal and ardor, and his matchless power of expression, occupies a foremost place of honor.

He was a product of the environment where he was born and raised, of the trials and tribulations of his long-suffering people, and of the Hebraic traditions which fed his spiritually-hungry soul. The poverty he had endured as a child, orphaned as he was from his father and none too tenderly raised by a stern and exacting grandfather, served to make him morally strong, forced him to learn to stand on his own feet. In his fine essay on Bialik Nahum Sokolow says of him: "In his childhood he was like a hot-house plant which grows under a glass, grows slowly, without a natural freedom of its own. His native powers fought to make their way into the open, but were forced to remain inside him. Yet they were not lost, but grew ever deeper and stronger". Bialik had many masters, and numerous were the

[105]

influences which affected his spiritual development: the Volozhin Yeshiva and the Haskalah, Zionism and Neo-Hebrew, "Hamelitz" and "Hatzefirah", "Ha-Pardes" and "Al Parashat Drakhim", Hassidism and Mitnagdism, the Besht and the Vilna Gaon, Moses Mendelssohn with his Bible translation and Nachman Krochmal with his "Guide", Mapu and Smolenskin, Mendele Mokher Sforim and Ahad Haam,—these and many others were his tutors and mentors; they formed and shaped his image, paved the way for him and made possible the very remarkable phenomenon known as Chaim Nachman Bialik.

Saul Tchernichovsky

To reminisce about Saul Tchernichovsky is, for me,
to evoke the warmest of feelings about one who was a truly
rare phenomenon in our Jewish life. Perhaps the one he
can best be compared with in non-Jewish literature is Oliver
Goldsmith, that naive and impractical Irish genius. All in
all, Tchernichovsky was an unusual embodiment of various
and often mutually exclusive aspirations and achievements.
By profession a physician and scientist who distinguished
himself as an army doctor in Russia during the First World
War, he was also a linguist who mastered many of the modern as well as the classical languages, from which he copious-
ly translated. But more than anything else his fame rests
upon his attainments as a Hebrew poet, notwithstanding
the fact that his use of Hebrew as a medium may be said
to have been a mere accident. His poetry, I am sure, would
have been no less impressive had he cultivated it in Russian
or in German—tongues in which he was thoroughly at home
and in which he also wrote, even if only on a limited scale.
Though a poet, Tchernichovsky remained a splendid physician, and his medical skill and scientific interests in no way
affected the quality of his poetry, or if it did it was only
to sublimate it and make it nobler and purer. Certain it is
that these two domains, science and poetry, did not rival or
antagonise one another in his case; they rather comple-
mented and acted as a stimulus one to the other.

What made Tchernichovsky into a Hebrew-writing poet?
The reasons for it are to be sought in the conditions of the
age in which he was born and reared. The sufferings of the

[107]

Jews and their struggle for survival in his native Czarist Russia; the Haskalah or enlightenment urge of his generation; the renascent Jewish nationalism which came in the wake of the fierce pogroms with which Alexander III began his reign—these and many other factors exerted their influence over the young writer and steered his pen away from the European languages and into the Hebrew channel.

Tchernichovsky became an ardent nationalist, though never a professional Zionist. Zionism, like Judaism itself, played no specially noticeable part in his life. He accepted both as a matter of fact, as something not to be questioned. He certainly was no fanatic, either in his nationalism or his religion, as is illustrated by his marriage to a Christian. The fact of his marrying out of the faith had absolutely nothing to do with the state of his Jewishness, nor with his creativity as a poet.

Physician though he was, it was Hebrew poetry which was his true calling, his daily bread. All the other occupations to which he devoted so much of his time, his medical researches and his philological studies, were merely avocations. He died at the age of 68, a young age considering that he never showed any inclination to yield to the illnesses that come with advancing years. But as a poet Tchernichovsky never grew old. The tempo of his work, his productivity as well as the quality of his writings did not grow less—perhaps it even increased with the years. Down to the very last he kept at his work, chiseling and polishing his verses, writing his inimitable sketches of Jewish life in Russia and of his experiences in the Czar's army, and translating from the masters of by-gone ages—until a cruel disease wrenched the pen from his hand and put an end to a most useful and industrious life.

One cannot write about Tchernichovsky and not mention

also his friend and collaborator in the Hebrew poetic field
—Chaim Nachman Bialik. The two had very much in common, even if their approach to Jewish life and problems
was markedly individualistic and often at variance. Both of
them belong to the same age and period of Jewish history
in Russia. The epoch, with its special conditions and problems, created them, shaped and moulded them, and they in
turn helped to shape and mould the age. They came from
two entirely different environments and were driven to the
same goal by two wholly different situations. Bialik came
from the Volozhin Yeshiva, the great fortress of rabbinic
learning; Tchernichovsky, from Heidelberg University with
its liberal traditions and critical outlook on life and religion. But they met on the common ground of Jewish national
reawakening. Their appearance before the Jewish literary
world occurred at almost the same time. Bialik's first poem
appeared in *Ha-Pardes,* in Odessa, in 1891; Tchernichovsky's
in Wolf Schur's *Ha-Pisgah,* in Baltimore, in 1892. Both began to write while in Odessa, and both finished their literary
careers in Palestine.

Bialik and Tchernichovsky were indeed brothers under
the skin in Neo-Hebrew poetry, the reverse and obverse of
the same literary coin. As writers they completed and com-
plemented each other, Bialik with his purely Jewish motif
and his prophetic zeal and fury, Tchernichovsky with his
"worldliness", the generally human and not exclusively
Jewish phase of his poetry. Actually, both were Jewish bards
more than anything else. For even Tchernichovsky in his so-
called "Greek" poems, like "Before the Statue of Apollo",
handles his themes as would a Jew who stands amazed at
the alluring "beauty of Japhet" and seeks to make his way
into the larger world. It is through his Jewish eyes that he
looks at the non-Jewish world. Tchernichovsky is no less

Jewish in his "Greek" poems than is Kohelet in the skeptical tone he assumes when proclaiming "all is vanity". We know that in the end he will assuredly come to the inevitable and purely Jewish conclusion of "Fear the Lord and keep His commandments".

In appearance there was much that was imposing about Saul Tchernichovsky, so that people would turn to look at him when he passed them on the street. He had, we may say, a feminine attractiveness. The first time I met him was in 1927, in Berlin, when he and Ben Zion Katz visited me at the Excelsior Hotel where I lived. Before me stood a tall man with a thick head of hair, a finely-carved dark-complexioned face and a pair of large dreamy eyes. Tchernichovsky looked the poet, as we imagine one. Not only the dishevelled mass of hair on his head, but his facial expression and his carriage gave indication of his being a man of the "upper spheres". But there was nothing of the poseur about him; it was all unconscious. He was extremely good-natured, affable, and, as already stated, terribly naive. Having just come from Palestine and Bialik, I was impressed with the difference in the external appearances of the two men. Bialik looked least of all like a poet. One would have taken him for a merchant—which indeed he was in his "off-hours"—a teacher, or manufacturer. Bialik also possessed much human shrewdness and intuition, as a result of which he was able to advance himself materially and was a man of means when he died, whereas Tchernichovsky remained poor all his life.

But notwithstanding his perennial economic hardships, Tchernichovsky retained his happy frame of mind, and was full of the joy of living. We met frequently that summer of 1927, took long walks through the ornate streets of Berlin's Charlottenburg, drove out to Grunewald and other fine residential suburbs, and ate at the "Medwed", at Kempinsky, and other good restaurants. The poet in him would reveal himself unexpectedly on many occasions. I recall how one late afternoon, as we sat in front of the Goethe monument near the imposing Reichstag building, he suddenly began to recite from Longfellow's "Hiawatha" which he had translated into Hebrew. His English pronunciation left much to be desired, but there was great pathos in the words he uttered, and showed how well one poet can fathom the spirit of a fellow-poet. I was profoundly impressed.

A year later, in the spring of 1928, I met Tchernichovsky in New York when he came in connection with a fund-raising campaign for Jewish educational institutions in Lithuania. This, too, was one of his weaknesses, as a result of his naivete, that he could not refuse to serve a seemingly worthy cause when approached; in consequence, he was often exploited. He spent much time in travel for a variety of Jewish causes, here in the United States and even in South America. By nature he was utterly unfit for any such work. He was a poor propagandist and very shy as a speaker. But his fame preceded him and served as a great attraction for the masses who flocked to hear him, or at least to see him. The campaign managers did the rest. I do not know with what success he met that summer in New York, but I well remember my frequent visits to his room at the Marie Antoinette Hotel and our many conversations and discussions. On one such visit, in the early afternoon, I invited him to accompany me to the meeting of the Association of Reform Rabbis which took place that day and at which I was to speak on "Tolstoy and the Jews". He agreed, and I introduced him to my colleagues of the Reform rabbinate of the Metropolis. In his reply he told of his reaction to what he had seen of American Jewry. He also stated that it was the first time

he had ever come before a body of Jewish "clerics", and
that he was wondering what people might think of it, and
whether many would not ask: "Is Saul (Tchernichovsky),
too, among the Prophets?" Later, he joined in the discussion
about Tolstoy in answer to what he heard me say in my address, as far as he could understand it from my English.
He himself spoke in German.

Eight years later we met again, in 1935, this time in
Tel-Aviv. Tchernichovsky was already a man of 60, but the
years had left little trace on him. He was the same gay,
care-free, and youngish-looking man, as ever naive and trust-
ing and ready to be exploited by friends and foes alike.
Accompanied by Dr. Isaac Silberschlag of Boston, we found
him in his little medical bureau on a side street in the already large and noisy metropolis of the Yishuv. He was then
in the employ of the Tel-Aviv municipality, if I am not mistaken, as attending physician in the public schools. I found
his tiny office a conglomeration of books thrown about in
disorder, and mixed in among them were bottles filled with
medicinal fluids and surgical instruments. There was an
accumulation of dust and the atmosphere was charged with
a variety of smells. It was clear: Tchernichovsky, with all
his interest in medicine, was a physician chiefly by trade,
as a means of earning a livelihood. Outside of his profession
he lived a life of his own in which the doctor was lost in
the poet.

And still another meeting with him in Tel-Aviv, our final.
It was a *Mesibah,* a sort of banquet tendered to me and two
other Hebrew writing colleagues from America by the "Hebrew Writers' Association" of Tel-Aviv. Tchernichovsky, as
head of the organization, presided and had something ap-
propriate to say about each of us; he also asked Dr. Shimon
Ginzburg, the secretary of the Club, to give a *Haaracha,* an

estimate, of our literary work. It was an eminently successful social affair, with many of the Palestinian writers present. Tchernichovsky, for once carefully apparelled, moved
among them like his namesake, King Saul, of old, towering
above them "from his shoulders and upward". His face was
beaming with inner contentment. I believe that he was never
happier than during those last years of his life that he spent
in Palestine. At last he had a sense of security and no worries about his daily bread. But the main source of his bliss
lay in the fact that he found himself among his own people
and that he was himself part of the wonderful experiment
of bringing life again to a people long dead nationally. At
long last, after a life spent in wandering from Odessa to
Heidelberg, to Petersburg, to Berlin, to Lausanne, the restless and fugitive bard found a resting place for his body
as for his soul in Palestine.

Aside from my elation over his fine physical appearance,
I carried away from my Palestinian meetings with him one
distinct impression: the manner of his Hebrew speech. It
goes without saying that Tchernichovsky spoke Hebrew not
only fluently but also correctly as to grammar and diction.
I am mentioning this circumstance in view of the fact that
there were many noted Hebrew writers whose Hebrew speech
was faulty and forced. Tchernichovsky, the polyglot, was
as meticulous about his speech in the old-new tongue as he
was when he spoke Russian or German. Yet one could not
but detect a certain artificiality in it, like an acquired language in the mouth of a foreigner. To me it sounded like a
foreign "accent", something which one would not find in
the speech of the Palestinian Jewish youth to whom Hebrew is a mother tongue. In this respect Tchernichovsky's
spoken Hebrew was more markedly artificial than it sounded
when coming from the lips of men like Shmaryahu Levin,

Vladimir Jabotinsky or Zvi Peretz Chayes. I explain it on the ground that the men I have just mentioned were eminent orators to whom speech came very easy, no matter what vehicle they employed. Tchernichovsky was not blessed with such a gift, and his Hebrew to that extent suffered.

But this observation need not be interpreted as a flaw, and I am mentioning it only by way of filling out the contours of this truly genial personality. Despite his failings as a speaker, Tchernichovsky remained the outstanding master of the Hebrew word. His style is wonderfully rich, colorful and elastic. It impresses one at once with its lightness and playfulness, and one cannot imagine, on reading him, that he had to work so strenuously and long before he could write with such apparent facility and ease. Few are the poets whose verses afford one such a genuine delight. In this he compares favorably with Heine or Longfellow—who, by the way, was one of his favorite English poets whom he gladly translated.

It is his mastery of the language which I find amazing and enigmatic. For unlike Bialik and others who were trained in the old-fashioned *Cheder* and *Yeshiva*, Tchernichovsky entered the world of Hebrew letters through the backdoor, so to speak. He never had to undergo the rigid disciplines of an educational system in which Hebrew was the one and only language taught, in the course of many years, in connection with Bible and Talmud studies. Bialik can be said to have known well no other language but Hebrew, if we except his native Yiddish; Hebrew was an integral part of his cultural self. Tchernichovsky, on the other hand, never saw the inside of a cheder. In his childhood he was sent to a "Russified" Jewish school where only a smattering of Hebrew was doled out to the children. Instead of studying Hebrew from the Bible or Talmud he was introduced to its rudiments through a "text-book", the *Gan Shaashuim* (Pleasure Garden), an imitation of Russian-language text books, composed by a man named Rosenfeld.

So far as is known, Tchernichovsky never studied the Bible for its own sake, and never looked upon a page of the Talmud. As a boy of ten he was attracted by the beautiful child-tales of Genesis which he read avidly with the help of Rashi. Then, when a little older in years, he read the Pentateuch with the aid of Mendelssohn's *Biur* (explanation), and his teacher also put into his hands the *Ein Yaakov*, a well-known work on Jewish ethical behaviour. The Hebrew literature of seventy years ago was extremely poor in juvenile books, and the lad read everything that came to hand of the few books available: Frischberg's heroic tales of the Davidian dynasty, Kalman Schulman's translation of Eugene Sue's "Mysteries of Paris", Mapu's *Ahavath Tzion*, Sokolow's *Ha-Asiph*, and the writings of Issac Bear Levinson. It appears that Hebrew lured him on just because of its quaintness, its atmosphere of mystery and mysticism, and though steeped in other studies in which Russian and German predominated, he decided on Hebrew as the preferred vehicle for his poetic labors. He was only 16 when he wrote his first poem which, as already stated, appeared in a Hebrew weekly published in America. It was a spring poem, which dwelt on the beauty of nature and the joy of the outdoors. The theme is old, but the manner of performance had a newness and freshness which gave promise of a great poetic talent in the making.

That first poem was an augury not only of the linguistic quality of the new poet's work, but also of its attitude towards the world. The note heard in it was new because it represented a new type of Jew. An emancipated Jew who turned his back upon the *Galuth*—the atmosphere of oppression and subjection and of accepted inferiority. Even as

nature enjoys its spring, so will the Jew upon emerging from
the winter of repression and persecution. A native of the
Crimea, and brought up in the Ukraine, Tchernichovsky
doubtless was inspired by the natural beauty of those fertile
parts of the Russian Empire. It implanted within him a spirit
of daring and courage which accompanied him throughout
his labors.

Again one is impelled to compare him with Bialik. In his
themes Tchernichovsky was no less "revolutionary" than
his great contemporary. He, too, was consumed with the passion of repulsion at everything that oppresses and enslaves.
The helplessness of the Jew embitters him, makes him very
unhappy. He reveals his state of mind in one of his earlier
poems, when he cries out for an "avenging sword" to get
even with his people's foes. It is, however, merely a cry of
despair, only an empty sound. He soon realises his impo-
tence. The age-old slavery had eaten into his soul, deprived
him of his wonted vigor and robbed him of his strength, and
all he can do in the end is "gnash his teeth and bite at his
chains".

He expresses the same thought, only more elaborately, in
a longer poem, "Baruch Mi-Magentza" (Baruch of Mayence), which is one of his finest creations. The Jew Baruch
tells of the catastrophe which befell the Jews of mediaeval
Mayence when the hoodlums fell on them, despoiled them of
all they owned, and murdered many of them. To prevent
Jewish women from being raped by the sadists, husbands and
fathers slaughtered their loved ones with their own hands.
Baruch, too, slays his two young daughters. He himself is
seized by the barbarians, he purchases his life at the cost
of his Jewish faith through baptism, and he is then thrown
into a monastery. There, in his cell, he finds time to think
of all that has happened to him and his, a spirit of revenge

overwhelms him, and snatching the burning candle off his table he sets the building on fire. The flames spread rapidly, envelope all of the monastery buildings and soon attack the city as a whole. Houses are burnt to cinders, human beings perish, mothers bewail the death of their children, and he, Baruch, now on the loose, meanders among the ruins of the conflagration he had caused. He finds consolation in the agony and sufferings he witnesses everywhere. Such, in brief, is the essence of this unusual poem which reminds one strongly of Bialik's "City of Slaughter" in which he chides the Jews for their timidity and cowardice in not offering due resistance to their attackers. Baruch does offer such resistance; at least he makes an effort to avenge himself on his people's enemies. But it should be borne in mind that Tchernichovsky's poem was written in 1902, thus preceding Bialik's poem by one year. The latter was not written until after the Kishineff massacre in 1903.

Saul Tchernichovsky introduced a new string in the lyre of modern Hebrew poetry, and one which found many imitators. His idylls of Jewish life, his nature poems, his nationalist songs, his matchless lullaby, his superb translations from ancient and modern poets, constitute in the aggregate a contribution to Jewish literature which render him immortal. As editor of a medical dictionary he greatly enriched the Hebrew terminology of the medical science, but it is as a poet that he excelled. I often think it a pity that so few of his poems have been done into English or even Yiddish (in this respect Bialik was more fortunate). He should by all means be made available to the larger reading public of the English speaking world. The task will not be an easy one, and it will require skilled artists to transmit the spirit as well as the beauty of his verse. The true savor of his writings one can find only in the original.

Zevi Hirsh Masliansky

ZEVI HIRSH MASLIANSKY, too, belongs to the Jewish celebrities of our age who attained distinction and fame by dint
of their native talents and their determined will to rise above
their obscure surroundings. Self-made men in the truest
sense, their number is surprisingly large among our people.
Mostly self-taught and almost self-raised, and arriving in
America penniless immigrants, they emerged from their
low estate to become leaders of Jewry who wielded a tremendous influence on their people's life and thought. In the
great Jewish community of New York none was more influential in his day than Joseph Barondess. B. C. Vladeck
gained the recognition of his fellow-citizens in America's
largest city where he held high public office, while Sidney
Hillman even became a political adviser to the President of
the United States. I could name scores of such men in many
a city who have come to my personal knowledge. Together
with their talents they also possessed the spirit which, in
most cases, held them so strongly welded to their Jewish
people whom they served so well. None among them, however, was more beloved than Zevi Hirsh Masliansky whom the
New York East Side and all of Yiddish-speaking America will long remember as the most distinguished of Yiddish pulpit orators.

Left an orphan by his father when a little boy, Masliansky
was forced to leave his destitute mother's home in Slutzk,
Russian Poland, and to spend most of his childhood and
youth in little towns where he attended *Cheder* and *Yeshiva*

and was taken care of by the good people of the community. The hardships of those years, instead of making him sour and rebellious, rather had a beneficent effect on him. It brought him close to Jewish life and to the virtues practiced in the patriarchal atmosphere of those small Jewish communities; it also enabled him to imbibe freely at the fountain-heads of Hebraic culture, the Bible, Talmud and other classical Hebrew works. As a mere youth he was drawn into the Haskalah (enlightenment) movement, and this led him, under the influence of Peretz Smolenskin, to the *Hibbat Tzion*, the forerunner of political Zionism. While serving as a Hebrew teacher in Pinsk, where Chaim Weizmann was one of his pupils, he showed promise as a public speaker and became a propagandist for the Zionist ideology, going from town to town where he addressed large audiences in the synagogues. Persecuted by the Czar's police which was ever keeping a watch on men of his type, he managed to slip out of Russia and for a time travelled through Western Europe and England, continuing his Zionist propaganda. He arrived in the United States in 1895 and, settling in New York, quickly became the inspiring leader of the already large and ever growing Jewry. But he did not confine his activity to New York alone; other cities throughout the American continent came to know and admire him. In his day Zevi Hirsh Masliansky was probably the most travelled Jewish preacher who was heard by more audiences than any other man. This is but a brief summation of the life-story of one of the most interesting men I have known.

I shall put down here but a few of my many recollections of Masliansky which will help portray him as the prominent figure and warm-hearted personality he was. I came to know him long before we became personally acquainted and formed the friendship which lasted until the day of his death in 1943. At the time Masliansky landed in New York he was a man in his early forties and I a mere boy of fourteen. Nearly all New York Jews at that time lived on the lower East Side which was in all respects a Jewish State, with a language of its own, Yiddish, with large daily newspapers, political parties, excellent theatres, and even rabbinical courts which dispensed justice among litigants. From the American point of view it was an exotic colony on the shores of America, a bit of Eastern Europe cast adrift along the East River in Manhattan. Even the policemen on their beats, who were Irish, couldn't help learning to speak Yiddish. It was a self-contained Jewry which took on the form of the East-European small town—and nearly all of those immigrants came from small towns which were the inexhaustible reservoir of the Jewish immigration. Their relations with one another were quite intimate, as is the case with people who belong to the same tribe. All had common interests, all were happy together over joyous events in Jewish life, and all were jointly mournful when bad news of pogroms and massacres arrived from across the seas. They also quarrelled among themselves over issues which to us today might seem rather trivial but to them were of paramount importance, like the supervision of Kosher meat, or the selection of a "Chief Rabbi" for the whole of the East side. The East Side Jews of fifty and sixty years ago did indeed live in America, but that was a mere geographical accident. Actually they still breathed the air of the Old World, and Kovno or Berditchev were closer to them than were Chicago, Philadelphia, or even New York City itself.

So when the Yiddish daily, the "Tageblatt", one day reported that the famous "Maggid" (preacher) Zevi Hirsh Masliansky had arrived and would soon begin his "Droshes" (sermons) in East Side synagogues, it became at once the great sensation of the day, and the topic of discussion in homes and wherever Jews gathered. To a great many of them he was no stranger. They had heard him in the old country and still remembered his inspiring and appealing words. But even those who had never known him were greatly interested, and all crowded to hear him. They were well repaid. They saw a tall, well-built man with a rosy complexion and a long beard who, though a Maggid, was yet entirely different from the usual run of Maggidim they had been accustomed to. He, too, made use of quotations from the Talmud and Midrash, but not just to display his mental acumen but rather to illustrate his thoughts and to strengthen the arguments he was pursuing. Unlike the other Maggidim, Masliansky never spoke of eternal damnation and never threatened with "Gehinom" (hell), even as he hardly ever mentioned the "Gan Eden" (paradise). His theme, with variations, was the Jewish national renaissance as made possible through Zionism, the self-redemption from the "Galuth" (exile) and the rehabilitation of Israel on his ancient soil in "Eretz Yisroel". He would constantly delve into the ancient lore of his people and skillfully draw from out of the past pictures and images which fascinated and thrilled. Gesticulation and mimicry came natural to him, and parts of his sermons he would sing in a rich tenor voice. In this way he would hold his audiences spell-bound for two or more hours. I believe that had Masliansky taken up acting for his vocation he would have made a first class star on the Yiddish stage.

I remember the very first sermon he delivered in New York, in the great synagogue on Norfolk Street which is still standing. The place was crowded to suffocation and huge masses of people who could not get in overflowed into the adjoining Grand and Broome Streets. Together with a

few other East Side boys I managed somehow to squeeze
my way in just as the police and fire departments had ordered the doors closed against new comers. When Masliansky arrived at the Shule he found his way blocked by a
solid mass of humanity. The police had to come to his as-
sistance and with their strong arms they actually carried him
in and placed him on the *Bimah* (pulpit). The then "green"
immigrant who was a highly emotional man was greatly
affected by this solicitude and reverence on the part of the
policemen and he spoke of it to the people, and later also
mentioned it in his memoirs. He reminded his audience of
the difference between Czarist Russia and free America,
and speaking of his own persecutions at the hands of the
Russian "Tchinovniki" stated: "Over there they would throw
me out of the synagogue; here in this blessed land they carried me in", and he asked his people to pray for the welfare and prosperity of America.

This happy experience of his on the very threshold of
his arival here was also the first étape in the process of
his Americanization. Let it be said that with all his devotion
to the Zionist ideal, in which he saw the one and only solution to the age-old Jewish problem, Masliansky never ceased
being an ardent admirer of the United States, and he kept
telling his audiences of the uncommon privilege they were
enjoying as residents and citizens of this land. Because of
his patriotic speeches in praise of America he was appointed
as the regular preacher of the Educational Alliance, a post
he held for a full quarter of a century. He continued his
Zionist propaganda from the same platform for he saw no
contradiction between Zionism and loyalty to America. For
me and numerous other young people of the East Side Masliansky was a pillar of moral strength to whom we flocked
for the inspiration of his addresses. His singing of parts of

his sermons in his melodious voice, aimed at making a special impression on his listeners, was most alluring. He would thus dramatize certain Biblical events and illumine the spiritual significance of heroes like Gideon and Hannah. The Bible under his touch came to life and appeared in a new and more beauteous light. Somewhat later in his preaching career he stopped singing, and I missed it greatly. He did it as a concession to America, where singing a sermon is not in style. Another concession, which I also regretted, was the gradual shortening of his fine long beard. Somehow, the beard was part of his spiritual stature and its final disappearance, except for a goatee, detracted from his masculine attractiveness, or at least I thought so.

He was a man of progressive ideas who sought to adjust himself to the American environment. Outwardly strictly Orthodox, it was really on his part mere conforming with inherited customs and life-long habits of religious observance. He had his own opinions about rites and ceremonies, and on the whole was kindly disposed towards all who differed from him, even on fundamental questions which he would defend with all of his gifted oratory but without rancor or malice. In his home he was the adored husband and father whose large family of children and grand-children would cluster around him as the patriarch which he was. To the outside world he was always the sympathetic and dependable friend ever ready to serve and help. When invited to speak in behalf of some charitable institution, he would himself be the first to contribute to the cause for which he was pleading.

In addition to his prominence as a preacher, Masliansky was also a writer of distinction in both Hebrew and Yiddish. He left several volumes of sermons and reminiscences in both languages, and his sermons have also been translated

into English (edited by Rabbi Abraham J. Feldman, in
1926). His diction in Hebrew was purely Biblical while his
Yiddish style was always excellent.

That Masliansky was a truly liberal-minded man can be
seen from his visit and address at the Hebrew Union College in the winter of 1898-99,—a most daring thing to do
for a Maggid who preaches in Orthodox synagogues. He
dwells on this event in his memoirs, and I can add a few
details to what he tells there, for I was then a freshman in
the H.U.C. and had much to do with his coming there.

Masliansky came to Cincinnati to deliver a series of
"Droshes" in the "Shules". When apprised of his arrival I
approached Professor Gotthard Deutsch and suggested that
the famous Maggid be invited to speak to the boys at the
Saturday afternoon Chapel services. Deutsch, always sympathetic towards the old school of thought and an admirer of
old-style "Maggiduth", consulted other members of the faculty and maybe even Dr. Isaac Mayer Wise himself, and
commissioned me and my brother, also a student there, to
bring the visitor to the College. As it happened, Masliansky
lived in a down town hotel not far away. It should be said
here, that if Masliansky was liberal-minded in his attitude
towards Reform Judaism, the College was no less so in inviting him. For Masliansky was noted for his espousal of
Zionism while the College, under the leadership of Isaac
Mayer Wise, was the citadel of anti-Zionism. To bring a
Zionist propagandist into the very sanctum of Reform was
indeed a rare occurrence. Yet it happened, and all concerned
were the happier for it.

How well I remember that momentous occasion! Masliansky wore his silk hat and his face shone as he was inducted

into the Chapel on the top floor where he was welcomed by the assembled professors and students. He was greatly interested in the services, in the student-choir and the sermon preached by one of the students. Towards the end came his turn to speak. Introduced first by Dr. Moses Mielziner and then by Professor Deutsch, Masliansky, who still could not speak English, and who was sensible enough not to resort to Yiddish in a place where he knew it was regarded slightingly, spoke in Hebrew in which, to tell the truth, not many of the students could follow him. They all were impressed, however, with the fervor and impassioned appeal of his words. He reminded the students of their happy lot as compared with that of the rabbinical students in the Yeshibot of Europe, where many of them were half-starved yet pursued their studies in spite of hunger and cold. Then he appealed to them to guard the "glowing embers of Judaism and keep them from extinction" when they left the College to become leaders in Israel. He then had the temerity to assail the extremist Reform rabbis of those days, Emil G. Hirsch and Moses Gries, who had gone so far in their radicalism as to remove the Sefer Torah from their Temples. It was perhaps indiscreet for him to make the attack in that place and in the presence of Isaac Mayer Wise himself. But he had the satisfaction of hearing from Dr. Wise's own lips that he fully agreed with him, for he was himself opposed to all such radical methods. Wise believed in reasonable and gradual changes in rites and rituals, and was surely not in favor of making the Jewish Temple resemble a Methodist or even a Unitarian Church. After the services he took Masliansky home with him, and the two had a very pleasant *Shabbas* chat.

Always on guard to serve the best interests of the Jewish people, Masliansky never declined an invitation to appear at mass meetings, or to serve on delegations and committees in connection with Jewish causes. I recall one day in the spring of 1919, in Brooklyn, my home town then, when Masliansky telephoned me to join him and a few others to call on Theodore Roosevelt in behalf of some undertaking to aid the Jewish victims of World War One. I do not recall the exact nature of the request, whether it was for Roosevelt to appear at a mass meeting or something else. T. R. received us very cordially at his office in down town New York, spent about fifteen minutes with us in friendly conversation, and regretfully declined the invitation. Masliansky was greatly disappointed but I consoled him that, after all, he tried his best. I also had occasion to witness his concern for the Hebrew writers of Russia and Poland who had been victimised by the war and had no one to help them. It was in no small measure due to his influence that Israel Matz of Brooklyn gave a large sum of money to establish the "Israel Matz Foundation" which looks after all such impoverished scholars, and he served on the Board of Trustees of that body from its inception to the time of his death in 1943.

As already stated, Masliansky, though an observant Orthodox Jew, yet was quite liberal in his interpretation of the customs and religious ceremonies of our people. This reminds me of my meeting with him in Jerusalem, in the summer of 1935, when he made me accompany him to the Temple Hill and the Mosque of Omar—something which the strictly Orthodox Jews of Palestine refrain from doing. It was Masliansky's second visit to the Holy Land and I found him and his wife living in a hotel in the new city that was rapidly rising through Jewish efforts outside the old walls. He had arrived there a few months before, and it was his plan to end his days in the land of his hopes and dreams. The Arab revolt of 1936-39 and the bloodshed it resulted in compelled him to change his plan, and he reluctantly yielded to the entreaties of his children and returned to America.

So I remember the joy which suffused his face when I surprised him that late July day in his hotel room. He had no inkling of my being in Palestine, and for him and his wife I was not merely an old friend but a living link with the happy American world they had left behind and with the children and grandchildren there for whom they were quite home-sick. He embraced and kissed me on both cheeks in European fashion. Our sudden meeting made the hearts of both of us more light, and wondrously beautiful as Jerusalem looked in all her mid-summer glory, she appeared to us even more fascinating at that moment. He insisted that we meet every day during my sojourn in the Holy City, and together we went visiting the historic sites, the Tombs of the Kings, the Hebrew University and the Agency Building. Masliansky took pleasure in serving as my guide, and though I knew Jerusalem quite well from my previous visits, I let him labor under the delusion that I needed his help, seeing that it made him happy.

One day as we were sipping tea at his hotel, he said to me: "Until now it was I who showed you around, but there is one place in Jerusalem which I would want you to take me to—the 'Har Ha-Bayit' (Temple Hill). Would you believe it that I have never been there, though I have been staying here now many months? I could not bring myself to act against the accepted tradition of our people, yet I want to see more than I can tell you the place where the *Bet Ha-Mikdash* (Temple) once stood. As you have already been there, you can help me in this. Alone I will not go, and not even with my wife, but with you I will take the chance. Do me this kindness".

I promised I would attend to it the next day. I ordered a taxi-cab which took us to the Mount of Olives, and from that side which is little frequented by people, we made our way, unobserved, to the Temple Hill, one of the most beautiful spots in the world. It was a terribly hot day, and both of us were greatly perspired, but we were oblivious of the discomfort and the exertion. Before us, on the flat promontory, was the enchanting panorama of shrines, arches and obelisks. Masliansky's face lit up with emotion, and there were tears in his eyes as in his voice. That was perhaps the noblest moment of his entire life. He who had spent a life-time talking about this very place and telling his people the numberless tales, traditions and sagas connected with it, at last was privileged to see it with his own eyes. But the place, alas, no longer belonged to Israel . . . At that moment he was both most happy and extremely wretched . . .

We entered the Mosque of Omar after going through the empty gesture (for 25 cents) of having our shoes encased in slippers to give the appearance of walking shoeless, as the rule required . . . . , and then made a meticulously careful study of the marvellous structure which occupies the very spot where once stood the Temple of Solomon; also the one built by Nehemiah and later rebuilt by Herod. We also descended below to where the "Foundation Stone" (or "Drink Stone", as it is also called), the stone on which the Temple rests and which served Masliansky so well in his sermons when he would inflame his hearers with the stories of the "Akedah" (the sacrifice of Isaac) and of Jacob's pillow when he slept in the open fields after running away from his parental home —which supposedly took place there. When we again emerged outside, we still lingered for some time in front of the building, our eyes feasting on that rare monument of architectural beauty and the huge expanse on which it stood. Then Masliansky grabbed hold of my arm and made me walk all over the place, asking numerous questions about the famous buildings that once stood there as mentioned by Josephus, like the Tower of Antonio, the Palace of Herod, etc., and to my regret I was helpless to gratify his curiosity. I had to confess to him that I did not know, but still he kept plying me with questions.

I believe this to have been one of the most memorable experiences of my life—and I have had many worth-while experiences—that terribly hot day when I walked around the Temple Hill arm in arm with the one-time Maggid of Lithuania who had become famous the world over as the fiery missionary of Jewish nationalism and the famous Yiddish orator of New York. There, on Jerusalem's lofty Temple Hill, we felt knit together as never before. Our hearts were filled with both sorrow and joy. We mourned for the ancient glory that had departed from us, but at the same time were as happy as never before because of the new dawn we saw rise for our long-tried people in its old-new land.

Isaac Mayer Wise

IT IS NOT EASY to write about Isaac Mayer Wise, for the very good reason that so much has already been written about him by his numerous disciples and admirers. Historians have devoted much space to him in their volumes, and his statue is to be found in the American Hall of Fame. One cannot speak about the evolution of Jewish life in the United States without mentioning this man who has, beyond a doubt, exerted the greatest influence on American Jewish life not only in his day but in succeeding generations. To this day he is still a living presence in every Reform Jewish congregation in the land, whether it is conscious of it or not. But precisely for this reason I cannot omit including him among my essays on the great men it was my good fortune to know. I knew Isaac Mayer Wise as well and as intimately as it is possible for a pupil to know his teacher, for I sat at his feet during the better part of the last two years of his life, from 1898 to 1900, and young though I was at the time, or perhaps just because of my extreme youth then, I could not but receive the full benefit of his spiritual influence. It is under the impact of that relationship between master and pupil that I am attempting this portrait of one of the leading Jewish figures of the 19th century.

Wise's many eulogists often spoke of him as the "Nestor" of American Judaism. Now Nestor was a mythological figure taken from a Homerian epic—a heroic character who was great both as a warrior and as an educator of the young, and who carried on as such to a ripe old age. This description fits Isaac Mayer Wise extremely well. He, too, was a warrior

who fought for his ideas and convictions, never laying down
his weapons until the day of his death; he was also a wise
and inspiring teacher of his generation who concerned himself mainly with the problems of the Jewish future and with
the religious education of the young. There was something
eternally young about him. When I first saw him in the fall
of 1898, he was already approaching his 80th year and physically not in the best of health—he was limping on one foot
—but this did not deter him from attending to the manifold
demands upon his time as rabbi of a large congregation, as
president of the Hebrew Union College, as editor of two
weekly periodicals, one in English, *The American Israelite,*
and the other in German, the *Deborah,* and as a civic minded
citizen who was active on the Cincinnati Board of Education
and other bodies and institutions. He would still accept invitations to preach in Christian churches where I had occasion
to hear him. Wise never sought to lighten his burdens as his
years were advancing. His congregation, true enough, gave
him an assistant for his Temple labors, but he always found
new problems to solve and new tasks to grapple with. His
main interest, however, was the Hebrew Union College which
he founded and where he was to be found every afternoon
regardless of the weather. It is well to note that for his work
in the College he received no remuneration. With him it was
a labor of love and a sacred opportunity which he would not
profane through accepting a material reward.

In the history of American Judaism Isaac Mayer Wise
will always be remembered for his work as a Reformer.
Some mistakenly regard him as the "founder" of Reform
Judaism, which is of course incorrect. No religious movement can be the work of any one man, be he ever so gifted
or brilliant. Only historic forces long at work can create
such a movement. Had Isaac Mayer Wise lived a century

earlier he would never have become the architect of the Jewish Reformation, nor would he have succeeded even in his day had he not migrated to America. We know that in its own birth place, Germany, the Reform movement proved abortive despite the outstanding leaders it had called forth, the Holdheims, the Geigers, the Jacobsohns and the Friedlanders, etc. In America it succeeded because the ground here was more propitious for the implantation and growth of the new idea. Long before Wise's arrival on these shores there had already been made an attempt to organise a Reform congregation in Charleston, South Carolina (in 1824). But it is likewise true that it took a man like I. M. Wise to fathom the possibilities of Reform in the New World. Even so, his was an up-hill struggle against numerous odds to which he might have succumbed but for his native optimism and a stubbornness which stemmed from his determination to keep fighting until victory was within his grasp.

My aim here is not to write the history of Reform Judaism in America but to touch on it insofar as it helps to bring into relief the personality of Isaac Mayer Wise. In connection with it I wish to say that there is more to be said about him than merely as the organising genius of the liberal Jewish forces in the United States which he undoubtedly was. He was also the ideological guide, the man who plumbed the depths of Jewish learning thence to bring forth teachings and principles to substantiate his claims for the validity of the Reform programme. In this he held his own alongside other eminent rabbis who came here from Germany and Austria-Hungary to become the prophets of the new religious orientation. The Einhorns and the Hirsches, the Adlers and the Kohlers—all were outstanding in their way, and each of them made a valuable contribution to the implanting of the seed. Some of them excelled Wise in scholarship and in eloquence. But he had the advantage over them that he refused to remain a mere propagandist from a cloistered ivory tower. Like Moses he came down to the people in the valley, spoke to them, taught them and organised and forged them into the mighty instrument they became for his Reform labors. But he did it all in the light of Jewish learning which he mastered and interpreted, and on the basis of Jewish tradition to which he constantly referred and which he harnessed to his Reform ends.

The better to understand the man, a few biographical data are in order. In himself Isaac Mayer Wise presented a rare phenomenon in the mere fact that he should have wanted to leave Europe for America not with the motive of making money in this land of opportunity, but for the sole purpose of continuing at his rabbinical vocation. Indeed, even from the standpoint of material success he might have done well in Europe where his gifts as a preacher, writer and communal worker surely would have brought him to the forefront of rabbinical leadership. But a man of his independent spirit could not be happy in the Europe of a hundred years ago where, in nearly all countries, including Germany and Austria and even England, Jews were still laboring under many grave disabilities. Born in 1819 in a small Bohemian town, Steingrub, of very poor parents (his father was a Hebrew teacher), young Wise devoted himself to Jewish and secular studies and in due time was ordained as rabbi by the rabbinical court at Prague which included among others the prominent Hebrew and Talmudical scholar and writer, Rabbi Solomon L. Rapaport. Not much is known of his academic studies. He attended the universities of Prague and Vienna but most likely never received a degree. No mention is made of it by any of his biographers, but this is a detail of little importance in the life of a truly great man.

Tired of Europe and its anti-Jewish atmosphere, probably tired also of his limited field as a rabbi in a little town called Radnitz, Wise, at the age of 27, already married and the father of a little girl, decided to go to America (1846). He went with the Jewish migration of his day, for it was the time when many thousands of German and Austro-Hungarian Jews took up the wanderer's staff and wended their steps to the New World. Two years later, with the collapse of the 1848 revolutions on which the Jews of the continent had pinned their hopes for full political emancipation, the little wave of 1846 was to become a mighty stream which included many more leading Jews and also rabbis of distinction, thus increasing the Jewish population he was to work with in later years. With his little family Wise stole out of Austria without a passport, and in Bremen boarded a sailing vessel which took 63 days to make the crossing. He landed in Castle Garden in New York with but two dollars in his pocket. Poor in money he yet was rich in hopes and happy in the prospect of the new life now opening up to him. He was as he states in his book of Reminiscences, "no longer an imperial-royal, Bohemian *Schutzjude*", but was "breathing a free atmosphere". This element of freedom, which was part of his spiritual being, should not be lost sight of. It was what made him rebel against traditional shackles which in themselves, as he believed, were of dubious moral value and had little or no support in Jewish religious fundamentals. It was what made him the great Reformer of American Judaism.

He had a thorny road to travel before he could detect signs of the triumph which he was ultimately to enjoy. He began his career as an American rabbi in Albany, N.Y., where he made his first attempts at reforming the ritual. Let it be borne in mind that the difficulties he had to encounter were not due to his pronounced views on matters of doctrine and principle so much as to his advocacy of changes in customs and ceremonials which he regarded as obsolete and out of place in the American environment. The Jews of Albany of 1846, like most American Jews of that time, were not noted for their Jewish learning. It would have made little difference to them whether or not their rabbi upheld the Thirteen Maimonidean Articles of Faith. They might have forgiven him his heterodox views of the origin and validity of many a rite and custom had he but agreed to leave all such ritual practices alone. But that, exactly, was where he, the aesthete, could not yield. To do so would have meant for him to compromise on and to interfere with the programme of the "beauty of holiness" which he had envisaged for his sublime Jewish faith. Wise aroused no little criticism, which turned to ill-will, among many of his congregation when he suggested the introduction of family pews, mixed choirs, and weekly sermons in German—the vernacular of most of the Jews of America in those days. Perhaps gradually they might have made their peace with these innovations, too, but when he sought to introduce such a rite as Confirmation of boys and girls—regarded by his opponents as an aping of Christian custom—and when he expressed the opinion that women should have the same right as men in making up the *Minyan,* or minimum quorum required for holding a public service, he brought down upon his head the condemnation and fury of the zealots. Rebellion against his ways and methods was smouldering and becoming more articulate from day to day. It came to a head on Rosh Hashana morning in 1850, at the divine services, just as the young rabbi was about to take the Scroll out of the Ark, when the president of the congregation, a Mr. Louis Spanier, advanced towards him and dealt him a vicious blow in the face. The congregation was horrified, pandemonium broke loose, and the people assembled in the synagogue took sides, for and against. A general fight ensued, the police arrived and arrested Wise, submitting him to the indignity of leading him through the streets to the station house where, however, he was immediately released. As a result there was a split in the congregation, and Wise went with the dissenters to head the new organization.

The echo of the slap administered to him on one of the holiest days of the Jewish calendar, right before the Ark of the Law, was heard around the entire American Jewish world and helped immeasurably to spread the fame of the courageous rabbi. It made a martyr out of him, and if the Orthodox cursed him, the progressives everywhere blessed him. Wise now became a national figure. Four more years he remained in Albany where he was now free to carry on his Reform experiments. In 1854 he was called to Cincinnati where Congregation B'nai Yeshurun elected him for life and where for forty-six years he labored zealously and with undreamed of success for the cause of Reform. His ministry in Cincinnati is the story of American Reform Judaism. There he displayed his unusual gifts as the great unifier of antagonistic factions, and as the organiser of institutions that still exist today. There he wrote his learned books and edited his interesting weeklies. Through him Cincinnati, a provincial Mid-Western city, became the spiritual capital of liberal Judaism and the College which he founded with so much effort and anxiety and nurtured and fostered with such tenderness and devotion, still basks in the sunshine of his fame, though it has grown into a much greater seat of learning and into a source of more far-reaching influence than even he perhaps could have foreseen.

If Isaac Mayer Wise discovered America as the new world where liberal Judaism could best flourish and thrive, he did not a little himself to make possible the realization of his hopes and dreams. He proved more effective than the other champions of Reform in the United States, because he was not only a theoretician but also a practical worker, prophet and priest at one and the same time. Alert, industrious, studious, he was able to make himself useful to the Reform cause in many ways. Exposed to the fire of its opponents, many of whom were men of considerable learning, Reform was in need of authority to prove its genuine Jewishness, and this Wise supplied in his writings and speeches. He was a facile and voluminous writer. Hundreds of his articles are scattered in the files of the *American Israelite* which he edited for more than forty years, and many a valuable bit of information can be found there to bolster his justification for one or the other innovation he advocated. But with it all he was far from radical in his interpretations. Compared with other Reform prophets of his day he could safely be described as a conservative.

In the course of his numerous arguments on the validity of Reform he pointed out that Orthodoxy, in the form it assumed in Europe was not necessarily based on fundamental Jewish doctrine, but was itself an outgrowth of the conditions that have for centuries hemmed in the Jew in the mediaeval ghetto. Judaism, when left to itself, breathes freedom and is best capable of revealing its full charm under conditions of political liberty. In his essay on "Moses, the Man and Statesman", he traces Reform principles to Moses himself. The laws and customs prescribed in the Pentateuch by Moses were adopted from the Egyptians and then assimilated to monotheism. To quote: "Whatever was useful in the traditions of his people and of the Egyptians, and congenial, he,

Moses, adopted and sanctioned. Evident wrongs which he could not dispose of summarily, e.g., polygamy, slavery, animal sacrifices, and similar existing evils, he modified and led to their gradual abolition".

Again and again he stresses the point that Judaism is by its very nature an evolutionary religion, that the element of growth and continuous adjustment is an integral part of its being. He sees this principle at play in the thinking of the very great teachers whom Orthodoxy itself has come to lean upon as its protagonists, men like Saadyah Gaon, Maimonides, Solomon Ibn Gabriol, Judah Halevi, Abraham Ibn Ezra, Joseph Albo, etc., down to Moses Mendelssohn with whom began the modern era in Judaism. The mere fact that those men under the impact of mediaeval Arabic philosophy, *speculated* about the nature of God and man's place in the scheme of creation, showed them to be progressive in the light of the times they lived in.

It is quite likely that in the days of his greatest struggle for his cherished convictions Isaac Mayer Wise was more stern and determined as an opponent than when I came to know him, though he was always chivalrous and gentlemanly towards his foes. In my day I found him to be a very mellowed old gentleman. Far from being set in his ways, I believe he was more open minded than ever. Thus, while staunch in his opposition to political Zionism which Herzl had launched a few years before his death, and while he fought the movement as strongly as he could—his onslaught on Zionism at the Montreal convention of the Central Conference of American Rabbis (1897) is a matter of record —he harbored at his own College professors with Zionist leanings. He showed his truly liberal attitude towards his ideological enemies in 1899 when the Central Conference met in his home city in honor of his eightieth birthday. Professor Casper Levias, of the Hebrew Union College, asked for the right to answer the attack on Zionism that had been made at this meeting. Wise, who was in the chair, not only permitted Levias to speak, but even suggested that he write out his answer in the form of a dissertation and that the pamphlet be published by and at the expense of the Conference. I was present at that meeting and like all the others who were there was greatly impressed. Had he lived today, and knowing what we all know of the tragedy of our people in the last two World Wars and of the hopes so many of us pin on Palestine and the Jewish State, I believe he, too, would have joined forces with all who looked Zionward for a solution of the Jewish problem.

I greatly cherish my memory of him as he appeared in those two last years of his life which I believe were, to us his students as doubtless to his congregation, the most inspiring of his entire life. There is something unusually appealing about an old man who holds on to the dreams and visions of his youth and to the last carries on with his public duties and functions despite the ravages wrought by time to his physique and in the face of the many disillusionments and frustrations which are the lot of even successful men. To see Isaac Mayer Wise at 80 shouldering his many burdens as though he were 50, and stubbornly holding to the course he had mapped out for himself sixty years earlier, was to witness a very rare and refreshing sight. In close proximity to him every day we, his pupils, far from losing any of our respect for him, only grew more reverential towards him. We saw in him a sage and prophet who preached the word of God out of his deepest convictions and who, if he loved all men, loved his own Jewish people best as the people of a great religious and ethical heritage. And we saw in him an ideal exemplification of the rabbinical calling which he himself loved so, and for which he held out the highest standards. Once addressing the student body at the opening semester of the Hebrew Union College, Wise laid down his idea of what a rabbi should be like. He said: "The morality of a rabbinical student, who seeks rabbinical honors from his alma mater, includes the possession of genuine religious zeal and enthusiasm. Without this he may become an actor in the pulpit, a polished elocutionist, a sensationalist, a seeker of plaudits, but no rabbi. I consider it my duty to admonish all present to leave this college if they lack religious zeal and enthusiasm, for they never will be honest rabbis; their whole life would be immoral. If you do possess this excellent quality you must cultivate it assiduously, so that it may become permanent in your character; you must be as conscientious in your religious practices as in your studies and in your fulfillment of all other moral duties".

As the years were piling up on him, Wise never considered retiring and seeking well-deserved rest from his labors. He lived the fullest kind of life, spending himself entirely in the cause he had espoused as a youth in his native Bohemia. His last Saturday morning in March, 1900, we still heard him preach in his pulpit at the beautiful Plum Street Temple he had built, and that Saturday afternoon we, his "boys" to whom he was a real father, still sat with him at the long table in the lecture hall of the old College building, reverently taking in his instruction and occasionally joining in laughter over some humorous remark or anecdote that came from his lips. And then came the stroke that felled him and brought on the end—a most dramatic finale in the life-story of a very remarkable man.

His death was universally mourned in America as in other parts of the globe. Eulogies about him were delivered in Reform Jewish pulpits in the length and breadth of the land. Many of the rabbis took for their text the classical lament of David for Abner: "Know ye not that a prince and a great man hath this day fallen in Israel?" (2 Samuel, iii, 38)—a most fitting description of Isaac Mayer Wise.

Gotthard Deutsch

IT IS WITH A SENSE OF CONSECRATION that I am approaching my task here of memorializing one to whom I was greatly attached both as a pupil and friend. In his life time Gotthard Deutsch was numbered among the great Jewish scholars of the age. He wrote a goodly number of books on a variety of topics and as professor of history at the Hebrew Union College exerted a considerable influence over many who today are leaders of Reform Judaism. Like so many other eminent men, the man Gotthard Deutsch was by far more interesting than the scholar or author. His books and articles are perhaps forgotten by now, but the man still lives in the memory of all who knew him, and notwithstanding his weaknesses he is still as dear to them today as of yore.

He was an exotic figure in American Jewish life in his physical appearance as in his mental processes. It may be said that he was a man of not a few contradictions. His Jewish name was Eliezer, but he called himself Gotthard, which is an inadequate translation into the German. His family name Deutsch (meaning German), well bespoke his deeply rooted attachment to the German "Kultur" which nurtured him spiritually all through life, even during the many years he spent in America. Yet he was first and foremost a warm-hearted Jew who never ceased interesting himself in everything pertaining to his faith and people. A Reform Jew by conviction, who in the classroom would often jestingly refer to Orthodox Jewish ways and customs at prayer, he nevertheless eagerly went to the old-fashioned synagogues in Cincinnati, where he would wrap himself in a *Talith* and chant and shake himself in the accepted manner of Orthodox tradition.

[143]

It is also worth recalling that though uncommonly tall and physically well-built, he was strikingly Jewish and rabbinical looking in physiognomy. His broad-boned face was encircled with a long beard which was nearly all white when I first met him, though he was then still under fifty. The beard and the spectacles over the heavily-browed eyes gave him the appearance of a rabbi or Hebrew teacher in a small town in Lithuania or Galicia. Yet this was only a superficial impression. Actually Deutsch was critical of the old Jewish ways, but he loved the externals of the old Ghetto life with all their flaws, and in his private life sought to hold on to them as much as his American environment would permit. He was at the same time sceptical of the future of Orthodoxy in America, and often expressed his doubts on this score in the classroom. Reason dictated to him that only Reform could thrive and perpetuate Judaism in the United States, and it was in that spirit that he brought up his children.

Because of his sentimental attachment to traditional ways in the face of American reality, there is reason to believe that Gotthard Deutsch was none too happy in his Jewishly-limited Cincinnati environment, and that he would have exchanged it gladly for a larger Jewish center had he been in a position to do so. It is certain that he was never happier than when on a visit to New York or Philadelphia, where he loved to meander in the Jewishly-inhabited districts, lose himself in the crowds, browse among the books in the Hebrew bookstores, and eat his meals in the Kosher restaurants. His greatest delight was to pass for one who was part of the Jewish life in the quarter he was visiting. I recall one hot summer evening some forty-five years ago, when he and I were promenading through the congested Galician Jewish quarter of New York's East Side. As we were making our way with difficulty through the crowds with their baby carriages and push carts, we were approached by an elderly gentleman with a dishevelled beard and cork-screw "peos" (side curls) who addressed Dr. Deutsch in his Galician vernacular. The man was evidently greatly perturbed over some domestic troubles and sought to unbosom himself to a fellow-Jew whom he mistook for a countryman from Tarnow or Prszemysl. He detained us in this manner some twenty minutes, and Deutsch not only lent him a sympathetic ear, but often injected a question and put up an argument in the same Yiddish dialect, so that the man never suspected that he was carrying on a conversation with one who was a noted German savant and, to boot, a professor in a "goyische" rabbinical seminary . . . The incident afforded Deutsch much satisfaction. It helped bring him once again closer to the soul of the Jewish masses.

As in so many other cases, Deutsch, too, owed his moral and spiritual development to home influence. But he was also a product of the Mendelssohnian enlightenment era and of the reformist tendencies of German and Austrian Jewry during his childhood and adolescent years. Born in 1859 in the small Moravian town of Kaunitz, he came of a family that gave many rabbis and Talmudic scholars to Austro-Hungarian Jewry. His father, though a merchant, was well grounded in Hebrew and Talmud and he was his son's first teacher. Young Deutsch gave early promise as a student, and when only nine years of age was sent to study at the Gymnasium of Nikolsburg. There he remained eight years, at the same time pursuing his Jewish studies under competent instructors. He then proceeded to Breslau where he entered the university and the rabbinical seminary, graduating from the former as a Doctor of Philosophy. His rabbinical ordination he received at the hands of the famous Rabbi Isaac Hirsch Weiss of Vienna. At first Deutsch devoted himself to teaching Jewish religious subjects in the Government school at Bruen, after which he became rabbi of the community of Bruex, where he remained four years. It was while in the latter post that Isaac Mayer Wise offered him the position of professor of history at the Hebrew Union College, in 1891.

I first met Professor Deutsch in 1898, a few months before I became one of his students, when he came to New York and paid us a visit in our humble quarters on Rutgers Street, in the Lower East Side. My brother, Jacob, had already been attending the H U C for a year and was greatly befriended by Dr. Deutsch. That explains his visit to our apartment that summer. It also throws light on the simplicity and cordiality of the man, and his interest in all young people who gave promise for future service to the Jewish cause. I was only 17 at the time, and it was his friendly attitude which encouraged me to decide to enter the College. Throughout the five years I spent in Cincinnati I found in him a friend who was ever ready to counsel and advise in the problems I faced as a student. He often entertained us at his home at meals where his wife, a true exemplar of a modern *rebbetzin*, excelled as a hostess. On all such occasions he would express his satisfaction at my work as a Hebrew writer, but cautioned me to be practical and to devote myself chiefly to the many phases of my rabbinical preparation, to insure a successful future in the ministry.

I recall my entrance examination at the Hebrew Union College when he and Dr. Moses Mielziner served as the examiners. Because I had applied for admission to the First Collegiate, which was then the fifth year, I had to prove my scholastic fitness for the higher class. Both those gentlemen, privately so kindly disposed, assumed a pose of great severity when they put me through the grinder. Mielziner opened a Talmudic tractate I had never before seen and told me to read at sight. The prospect of failure frightened and unnerved me, but I noticed my old friend "Rashi" there, the ubiquitous commentator of the Bible and the Talmud, and I clutched the life-line he held out to me. Turning to my examiner I asked whether he would object if I consulted Rashi before rendering the translation. The good old Doctor smiled and reassured me that that was just what he wanted me to do. With the aid of Rashi the test proved none too difficult. Deutsch showed himself even more stringent in the Bible test to which he subjected me. In addition to reading at sight in places he picked out at random he also asked me to explain orally the meaning of certain archaic words in Isaiah and Job, and also to tell where they were to be found. The impression I got was that he was out to "trap" me. I escaped the snare through a sheer psychological device. The very rareness of the words had impressed themselves upon my memory more than would have been the case with more common words, so that I readily located them. Later, after being at the College for some time and noting that the average student's Hebraic knowledge was rather limited, I began to wonder why Dr. Deutsch had made it so hard for me, and one day I asked him about it. He answered that he did it because he expected more from me than from others, adding with a smile that it happened so seldom for him to give an entrance exam to one who was a contributor to "Haschiloah" (my first essay in that celebrated monthly appeared that summer), and that he was greatly enjoying himself in the process . . .

Distinguished though he was as a scholar, Deutsch was not any too succesful as a teacher. As already stated, his specialty was Jewish history, and with his great knowledge of the subject he should have been able to do uncommonly good work with his students. The subject is perhaps of greatest importance for a rabbinical student. Himself a pupil of that prince of Jewish historians—Graetz—Deutsch had much to give to his students. Actually he gave them very little, and I got the impression that he came into the classroom insufficiently prepared for his work—something which students quickly sense . . . He would make a few superficial observations and mention some dry data in connection with such world-shattering events like the expulsion from Spain, the Chmielnitzky massacres, or the Messianic and pseudo-Messianic movements. At times the lecture, if it could be called that, would take on the form of reading several events with dates out of a little notebook. It happened that simultaneously with our attendance at the H U C we also studied at the University of Cincinnati where we took work in mediaeval and modern history from so distinguished a historian as P.V.N. Myers, who was noted for his several books on the subject that were used widely in colleges throughout the country. Dr. Myers would keep us spell-bound by his lectures on the renaissance, the Reformation or the French Revolution. He appeared to us like an inspired prophet who opened up new vistas of worlds long passed, and helped us understand the world we were living in. The contrast between him and Deutsch was too marked not to be noticed by us.

Yet I would not want to convey the impression that he was altogether ineffectual as a teacher. On the contrary, I believe that Professor Deutsch was perhaps the one man on the College faculty who exercised the greatest influence on his students, but he did it in his own way, a way not usually known or practiced in American colleges. His was a sort of "Socratic" method of teaching. Instead of giving formal talks on a given subject, he would convey information in a round-about, indirect and conversational manner. The "lecture" proved to be no lecture at all but a friendly and often intimate chat on things Jewish. Sometimes the discussion had nothing to do with the lesson we were supposed to receive on a given topic. Instead of learning about, say, Sabbatai Zevi or the Hassidic movement, we would get his opinion on Zionism or on Neo-Hebrew, on Zangwill or Judah Leib Gordon, and it was an opinion worth hearing, accompanied as it was with humorous tales about the life, the habits or experiences of many a prominent Jew. Deutsch infected us with his own love for things Jewish, even if we did not carry away from him any definite views and ideas about Jewish history in its totality. Many of us made up for it by going to the works of Jost, Graetz and others. Meeting with Deutsch in the classroom was always a delightful social and cultural experience.

Deutsch's main interest lay not in teaching but in writing. He derived his greatest pleasure from seeing his books or essays in print. And in his writings, as in his "lectures", he was a *causeur*, informally talking on this or that subject, often bringing in extraneous and irrelevant matters and seasoning it with jokes and anecdotes. Everything was grist for his mill, just so it had something to do with Jews and Judaism, and he wrote in several languages, English, German and, occasionally, also in Hebrew. I do not recall that he ever attempted writing in Yiddish, though he was a constant reader of the American and European Yiddish press and often corresponded with leading Yiddish writers. Every day he would spend several hours at his typewriter, pounding out articles for the *American Israelite,* for which he wrote a weekly column, the New York *Staats Zeitung,* the Berlin *Allgemeine Zeitung des Judentums,* or the *Deborah,* the German-language weekly which Isaac M. Wise edited and which Dr. Deutsch took over after the former's death in 1900. His books, which he also wrote in German and English, cover a variety of topics, from studies in Biblical archeology and in theology to text books on history, dramas, and novels. As a writer he was uncommonly prolific, and therein lay his greatest weakness, for instead of concentrating on a specific field of knowledge he split his talent in too many directions. One got the impression that he wanted to demonstrate his versatility. The man who delved into the science of Judaism with such works as "Symbolik in Cultus und Dichtung bei den Hebraern", "Paradigmentafeln zur Hebraischen Grammatik", "Epochs of Jewish History", "Theory of Oral Tradition", "Philosophy of Jewish History" and others, also invaded the realm of fiction with novels like "Andere Zeiten" and "Unlesbare Fesseln". He had great faith in his literary powers along all lines of creative endeavor. I recall his telling us one afternoon of a novel he had just published in English which he regarded as quite meritorious because, as he pointed out, it was written in full conformity with all the rules that govern such writing. In this he was right. The book was indeed a true specimen of compliance with the rules and regulations of literary craftsmanship. But in addition to keeping up with the rules one must also have talent as a fiction writer, and it was just this one little thing Deutsch lacked.

If only he had limited himself to his own special domain, that of Jewish history, he surely could have made a mighty contribution to a subject than which there is none more fascinating or vital to the understanding of the development of the Jewish people and of the world as a whole. With his knowledge of Greek and Latin and his accessibility to the sources of ancient and modern history, Gotthard Deutsch might have succeeded in throwing new light on many an obscure corner in the history of Israel's pilgrimage through the ages. But he lacked the patience indispensable for creative research. The ephemeral lured him more than the perma-

[150]

nent, details appealed to him more than the over-all picture, and he failed to see the forests for the trees. He possessed a remarkable memory for facts and dates, and at his death left a monumental literary legacy, his card-index, covering some 70,000 items, names and events which should prove very useful to all students of Jewish history.

Aside from his attainments as a man of great culture, Deutsch also had much social charm. He was an interesting conversationalist, and was a center of attraction wherever he went. At the annual conventions of the Central Conference of American Rabbis, which he never failed to attend, and where he often delivered learned dissertations, he was a most popular figure.

His last years were stormy ones, and I believe he was not a little affected by the upheavals attendant upon the First World War and its fatal outcome for the country he was so reverently attached to—Germany. For Gotthard Deutsch Germany was still the land of poets and thinkers, of a great and mighty culture from which the whole world benefited. He could not make peace with the idea that the land of Lessing and Klopstock, Kant, Goethe and Schiller, could possibly be in the wrong in fighting so patently barbarous a foe as was Czarist Russia. The truth is that most thinking people among the Jews of the period—and not a few of the non-Jews—felt the same during the early years of that conflict. It was not until the Lusitania incident that Germany began to show herself as capable of a cruel barbarism of her own. Hatred of Russia made us all side with Germany, overlooking the fact that highly civilized powers like Great Britain and France were also involved. Deutsch was most ardent in his sympathy with Germany, for to him it meant the land to which he was so greatly indebted for his education and the many cultural values which she had afforded him.

The entry of the United States into the war caused a revolution in the thinking and feeling of the American people. Gotthard Deutsch was left high and dry on the limb of his attachment to what was now an enemy nation. His life-long love for Germany prevailed over his sense of duty as an American citizen, and he had the temerity to repeatedly condemn the step taken by this country. This exposed him to no little censure, and at one time he came near losing his post at the College. At the last moment wiser counsel prevailed, and he was retained in his professorship, but the episode had a devastating effect upon his spirits and undoubtedly affected his health.

He survived the war only some three years, dying in 1921 in his 63rd year. In his will he provided that no eulogy be delivered at his funeral service, which was to consist only of prayers and the reciting of psalms he himself had selected. It provided also that he be cremated. This, too, was in contradiction with what I believe were his personal predilections for the conventional burial. He often had pointed out to me the pictures of his father's and mother's graves which hung on the wall of his study. It is evident that here, too, his reasoning as a Reform Jew prevailed over the traditional religious sentiments which he cherished.

Among the images of the past in connection with my Cincinnati school years, that of Gotthard Deutsch stands out in greater relief than any other. And every time I get to that city on the banks of the Ohio—and I do it often—I think of him and miss the good friend and amiable teacher of half a century ago. The man with the cordial smile and large friendly eyes is not there, and Cincinnati does not look the same city to me.

Solomon Schechter

To WRITE ON SOLOMON SCHECHTER is to bring into relief a most colorful personality and one that played an unusually prominent part in the unfoldment of modern Jewish history, more especially in the United States. It may well be said that Dr. Schechter was himself an important chapter in that history, one that he wrote with his own hand, a chapter which began in the Old World where he spent 53 years of his life, and ended in America where he finished his eventful career after a residence of 13 years. He was both a scholar of the first magnitude who left an indelible mark on the world of letters and of scientific research, and a leader of Jewry whose influence is felt to this day in the religious life of our people. As a scholar he belongs chiefly to Europe where he won his spurs and made a distinguished name for himself; as a leader of the organised religious forces of Jewry he belongs wholly to America.

He was indeed a rare combination of the old and new type of Jew, the Yeshiva Talmudist who was thoroughly at home in the vast Hebraic literature of all times, and the modern scientific researcher who stood at the forefront of the academicians of his day and was sought after as teacher and lecturer by many of the leading universities of England and America. It is wonderful to contemplate how the Hassidic *Yeshiva Bochur* (student) of a small town in Roumania, with the long Kaftan and curly side-locks, developed into the world-renowned Professor of Rabbinic Literature of England's proud Cambridge University, who at one time focussed upon himself the attention of the entire world of scholarship by his Geniza discoveries. From little Fokszany in the backwoods of uncultured Roumania to a seat of learning as famous as Cambridge is quite a leap which, however, the one-time unlettered and penniless boy seems to have made without too great exertion. From Cambridge to New York and to the foremost leadership of American Jewry, already presented less of a hurdle. That the product of the Roumanian Ghetto should have become so distinguished a master of English as to rank among the best stylists in that tongue in the England of his day—notwithstanding that he began to study the language quite late in life—is an enigmatic performance such as, it seems to me, only we Jews are capable of.

Solomon Schechter was unusual also by his mere physical appearance. Tall and well-built, though stooped from bending over countless tomes, he possessed a leonine head, and a dishevelled growth of beard which encircled his full rounded face. His physiognomy was not only physically attractive but expressive of spiritual energy and moral firmness. His was a face which a Rembrandt would give half a kingdom to be able to paint. A rabbinical face, it denoted in addition to Jewish self-esteem also inner conviction, self-control and faith in his own powers. As we shall see in the course of this essay, Schechter was one of the few whom life favored in many ways: he rose in the scale of success largely through a sequence of fortunate accidents. Yet I believe that he would have attained to the heights even without those accidents, perhaps even without Cambridge and New York. He possessed character such as enabled him to overcome all stumbling blocks. He, too, had to struggle for his very existence and for his life as a scholar. But where others might have succumbed, Schechter simply found in his hardships an added incentive for his efforts.

[154]

His life-story reads like a leaf out of the book of the old-time *Maskilim* (self-educated, enlightened Jews) of Lithuania or Poland, notwithstanding that his own cradle stood in an out-of-the-way place in Roumania, far removed from the centers where the Haskalah exerted its greatest influence. Born in 1849 in Fokszany of parents who originated from Volhynia, Russia, his father, who had left the Czar's dominion in order to escape serving in the army, was a follower of the Hassidic group that was led by Rabbi Schneor Zalman, and it was after this famous rabbi that our hero was named. There were five other children and the father had difficulty in supporting his family from his trade as ritual slaughterer (hence the name "Schechter" he adopted) of the community. Little Schneor Zalman never went to *Cheder*, perhaps because there were no worth-while *Melammedim* (teachers) in town. His father, who was well-versed in Bible and Talmud and a devout and warm-hearted Jew, took personal care of his son's education. At the age of 3 Schneor Zalman already knew the Pentateuch and gradually he advanced to the Prophets, the Talmud and Midrash. At 10 he ran away from home to a near-by town where there was a Yeshiva. Brought back to Fokszany, he again absconded, and this time he remained away several years. Because there weren't enough Hebrew books to go around among the pupils, Schneor Zalman had to content himself with learning his Talmud and rabbinic works by heart, and in the process acquired a powerful memory. The Talmud furnished him not only with a remarkable legalistic system but also a glimpse into Jewish history, and the many tales and legends of Jewish historical events and heroes make a lasting impression on the lad's mind and he is lured on to learn more of that history. Roumania is an Antisemitic land where Jews are constantly persecuted, and when he is 12 years old he by chance comes across a Hebrew translation of Josephus' booklet against Apion, the Greek Antisemite of the first Christian century, and he thus discovers that Antisemitism had its ancient roots, going back to pre-Christian days. With this book, according to his biographer Norman Bentwich, begins a turning point in Schneor Zalman's life. He soon finds other Hebrew books which were taboo among the strictly Orthodox, even such works as Maimonides' *More Nebuchim* and De Rossi's *M'Or Enayim*, and he reads and studies them clandestinely, also the Hebrew newspaper *Ha-Maggid*. Schneor Zalman is well on the way to becoming himself a Maskil.

But he has more luck with his Haskalah than the Yeshiva Bochurim of Poland and Lithuania of the same period whose urge for world culture made them targets of severe censure and condemnation. Schneor Zalman is not persecuted, and he even succeeds in making his way out of the Ghetto and to satisfy his thirst for knowledge in a few of Europe's leading institutions of learning. True, it takes many years before his aspirations are realised, and when he leaves his native town for the outside world he is already a man of 24. But perhaps that, too, was necessary for the making of the complete Schechter. It meant that many more years of study of the old masters, so that he became most erudite in all branches of Hebraic learning and culture. In the meantime, too, there happens to him what happened to so many other Jewish young men of the time. His pious parents force him into a marriage in keeping with Orthodox tradition which says that no man should remain single once he is an adolescent. Our hero is only 17, and the match turns out unhappily and is terminated with a "Ghet" (divorce) a year later. The incident causes much mental anguish to the sensitive youth, so that it takes him more than 20 years to overcome its effects. It is not until he is a man of 40, and already a renowned professor in a great English university, that he again ventures out upon the matrimonial sea. This time the marriage is highly successful. The Mrs. Schechter we all knew in America was a charming and lovable woman and a true helpmeet to her distinguished husband.

Four countries, apart from the United States, shared in the making of Solomon Schechter. Roumania gave him the foundation for his Jewish culture, unsystematised though it was, and the large measure of attachment to his Jewish people which distinguished him. In Roumania he also got a first-hand knowledge of the blind and unreasoning Jew-hatred which obsessed that land. The realization that he was a step-child in his native land where, as a Jew, he faced a dismal future, leads him to emigrate and he arrives in Vienna where, under the guidance of eminent men like Isaac Hirsch Weiss, Meir Friedman and Adolph Jellinek he learns to systematise his knowledge and to use it profitably for himself and for the literary world. He remains in the Austrian capital six years, supporting himself as a teacher in Professor Friedman's home and as custodian of Dr. Jellinek's large library. When Vienna has nothing more to offer him, he again takes up the wanderer's staff and lands in Berlin where he matriculates in the university and in the "Hochschule", noted rabbinical seminary. In Berlin he comes in frequent contact with men of scholarly renown like Professor Moritz Lazarus, Leopold Zunz, Moritz Steinschneider and Israel Levy; also with two famous non-Jewish professors at the university, Zeller and Mommsen. Berlin is still the capital of the *Wissenschaft des Judentums* (science of Judaism) and to it flock seekers of Jewish knowledge from all parts of the globe. Berlin is at the same time also the heart and nerve

[157]

center of "Cultural Antisemitism" and our Schechter is treated to the unpleasant picture of men of high academic learning devoting themselves to an inquiry into the so-called *Judenfrage* (Jewish problem) which they themselves helped call into being and which they seek to explain on "scientific" grounds. This does not mean that they are motivated to get at the truth but rather that they are looking for a justification of their anti-Jewish prejudices and their animosity towards Judaism. To this end they probe into the history of the Jews and their literature, the Bible and the Talmud. From this stems their so-called "Higher Bible Criticism" when they dissect Scriptural verses and sentences for the purpose of casting aspersion on the Jewish spirit by contrasting it with that of Christianity. Our Schechter sees it all, hears what is going on in the higher academic spheres of cultured Germany, and reads the Antisemitic sermons which Court Chaplin Stoecker delivers in the presence of His Majesty, the Kaiser. The poor man is aroused to a high pitch of fury at his people's traducers, and would eagerly take a hand in answering them, but his hands are tied. He is a stranger in the land, a foreigner who lives there by the grace and kindness of the Police Department. Besides, he knows he is not yet quite ready for the task. He still requires time and more study in preparation for his life's work. That was to come a few years later, when he was to find an asylum in a friendly and democratic England, where he was to become a foremost authority of his day on the ancient literature of his people.

It was his sojourn in the Prussian capital which determined his entire future. Among those who migrated to Berlin in quest of Jewish knowledge was a young British Jew, Claude G. Montefiore, a scion of the prominent Montefiore family, who arrived there with his sisters to attend the lectures at the "Hochschule". He also wanted more immediate help in his studies by a competent instructor, and Solomon Schechter was recommended for the job. This had a far-reaching effect in the first place upon Montefiore himself, for it was from Schechter that Montefiore got his insight into ancient Jewish life and literature which served him so well when he came to write his books on the origin of Christianity and on the New Testament. Let it be said here that Montefiore and Schechter were worlds apart in their interpretation of the Gospels and in their attitude towards Judaism itself. Montefiore was radical in his evaluation of Judaism's position in the modern world, and in course of time became the founder of the Reform Jewish movement in England. Schechter's liberal attitude never went further than what is known today as the Conservative view-point, which indeed he spearheaded in the United States when he came here to head the Jewish Theological Seminary. Yet the two men remained staunch friends all through life, and it is certain that it was their happy relationship while in Berlin which led to Schechter's subsequent good fortune in England. When Montefiore's time came to return home he offered to take his tutor with him that he may continue his studies with him. Schechter grasped at this opportunity which opened up a vista of a care-free existence. It meant access to the great libraries of the British Museum, of Oxford and Cambridge, and it was to lead to a phenomenal career in which Schneor Zalman of Fokszany became the great Doctor Solomon Schechter of England and America.

It will require much more space than I have at my disposal to dwell at any length on Schechter's life and work in England, the zeal and energy with which he threw himself upon the thousands of books and manuscripts he found there which tell the story of the Jew and of Judaism of 4000 years ago, his wonderful progress in the use of the English language in which he acquired a classical style notwithstanding that his accent was so markedly foreign when he spoke it. His many essays which he published in distinguished British and American journals and which subsequently appeared in book form in a number of volumes, constitute a most valuable contribution to the understanding of Judaism, and I do not know of another Jewish savant who so popularised Jewish knowledge in English as did Schechter in the three volumes of his "Studies in Judaism", or his "Aspects of Rabbinic Theology". He also wrote brilliantly on non-Jewish topics, and his essay on Abraham Lincoln, in which he dwelt on the mystic element in the character of the Great Emancipator, is one of the best ever written on the subject. His literary activity continued for thirty years, until his death in New York in 1915, and the list of his published works is long, consisting mostly of manuscripts, and fragments of Talmud and Midrash which he edited. But what makes him an all-time immortal in the history of Jewish letters is his discovery, in 1896, in the old "Geniza" of Cairo, of the Hebrew original of the book of Jesus Ben Sira.

Because this discovery is the high-water mark of all his achievements and led to the creation of a whole literature on Ben Sira and other works he had unearthed in the Egyptian Jewish quarter, it is imperative to devote a few minutes to it. With this discovery Schechter demonstrated that mere knowledge, howsoever vast, in itself is not enough. The truly creative scholar is one who is in love with the subject of his studies close to his heart, so that he will undertake venturesome and even perilous journeys for its sake—just as will a true lover on behalf of his beloved. Solomon Schechter never was a dry-as-dust scholar, but one whose chief interest in life was to understand the cultural heritage of Judaism and of the people that brought it into being. And the more he studied the ancient literature of his people the more his interest grew in the people itself.

Here, too, luck attended him—a lucky accident. For it is conceivable that Solomon Schechter might never have heard of the Geniza and its contents but for the fact that two Christian ladies of his acquaintance had returned from Egypt with two old and dusty sheets they had picked up there by chance. They brought their find to the learned man, now already comfortably established in his Cambridge professorship, to pass judgment upon it. Schechter at once recognised the one sheet as a fragment of the Jerusalem Talmud. The other fragment, too, seemed familiar. He thought it was an imitation of the Book of Proverbs (which the Book of Ben Sira indeed is). He was already acquainted with the Hebrew translation of Ben Sira which had been made from the Greek, but the fragment he held in his hand was different in style from the translation. His trained scholar's eye told him it must be something very important. To satisfy his curiosity he went to the library where he re-read the English translation of Ben Sira and compared it with the sheet he was holding. This convinced him that it was part of the Hebrew original. He at once communicated his find to the world, and soon thereafter set out for Cairo to search for the rest of the manuscript.

It was not an easy task. It could be compared with the difficulties encountered by a scientific expedition to the North Pole or the Equator. The "Geniza" was a walled-in chamber in one of the old synagogues of Cairo where for more than a thousand years were dumped all sorts of written and printed matter. Some were of great literary value, others mere pieces of paper or parchment absolutely worthless. In order to get to the pile of rubbish it was necessary to break through a wall and then to labor in the extremely hot atmosphere which was heavily laden with bacilli and the dust of many centuries. But that wasn't all. To be able to get to the Geniza at all one had first to obtain the permission of the rabbis and trustees of the community and also the protection of the British administration. Not a few of the contents of the Geniza had been stolen and sold to speculators, and our poor Cambridge scholar had to hand out *baksheesh* right and left to redeem those precious objects. For weeks on end he labored in that oppressive atmosphere and in the end his health was seriously impaired. But he attained his goal. He emptied out the whole of the Geniza into 30 sacks which he despatched to England. When the treasure arrived at Cambridge University it became the great sensation of the day. The university authorities assigned a special room for the study and research that was to follow, and Schechter's name became a familiar item on the front pages of the world's newspapers. After a period of rest and recuperation in Palestine Professor Schechter returned to tackle the huge task that was before him, that of examining the mountain of antiques he had brought out of their Egyptian grave. The result was not only a completed original Ben Sira but other important works bearing on ancient Jewish history. In recognition of this stupendous achievement Cambridge University made Schechter a Doctor of Laws.

Solomon Schechter's work in the United States is in itself a most important chapter requiring special treatment, and I shall not go into it here. It will suffice to state that he occupies in the Conservative movement in American Judaism a place not unlike that occupied by Isaac Mayer Wise in the Reform movement. The Jewish Theological Seminary of New

York which he built up from a small and poorly equipped school into a great seat of Jewish learning is his everlasting monument, and it is still called after him, the "Schechter Seminary".

With all his conservatism, and the not infrequent strictures he passed on Reform, Schechter was a liberal minded man who could see and appreciate the opponent's view-point. He was far from being a zealot. I recall hearing him at the dedication exercises of the new Hebrew Union College buildings in Cincinnati in 1913, when he was given a tremendous ovation by the leaders of Reform Judaism headed by Dr. Kaufman Kohler, the then President of the H.U.C. The gist of Dr. Schechter's remarks was to the effect that there was room in Judaism for various schools of religious thought. Having come from England he knew the meaning of having an "opposition to His Majesty's Government", an opposition which is loyal to the country and labors for its best interests according to its lights and convictions.

But he remained rooted in his own old-fashioned Jewish world, the thought and influence of which dominated him to the last. And he was likewise a staunch adherent of the Zionist ideology, though not active in the movement for the Jewish nationalist revival. To this day there lingers in my memory my visit to his summer home in Tannersville, New York, in 1908. I went to him with a good-sized delegation from the Zionist convention which was held there that summer. We went to him as on a pilgrimage, and the good Doctor and his hospitable wife met us at the door and bade us welcome. Despite his sixty years Dr. Schechter looked hale and fit, and was in excellent spirits. Mirthful tales and anecdotes rolled from the lips of the man with the patriarchal face and disheveled beard, and moved us all to laughter. Refreshments were passed around and he himself waited on not a few of us. All at once he began to sing Hassidic Zemiroth (songs) and Jewish folk songs in Yiddish, among them the well-known and popular "Oifn Pripetchok" which we all sang along with him, especially the refrain "Kometz, Alef O" which we joined in as a chorus. We saw him in an entirely new light, but perhaps it was the old light of his obscure past in the far away days in Old Roumania.

Before us stood not the eminent President of the Jewish Theological Seminary, the one-time Professor of Rabbinics at Cambridge, and the famous discoverer of the original Ben Sira, but the Yeshiva Bochur of old. Doctor Solomon Schechter at that moment reverted to the type he liked best, that of Schneor Zalman of Fokszany. It is as such that I prefer to remember him. In that group of Zionists and Hebraists, dreamers of their people's national resurrection, Solomon Schechter found himself at home more truly than in the aristocratic world to which fortune had consigned him.

Henrietta Szold

SHE, TOO, belongs to the great Jewish personalities of our age whom it was my good fortune to know personally and well, and for this knowledge and the friendship that went with it I am most grateful, primarily because of the moral influence it had on my own life. It was impossible to know Henrietta Szold. and not be influenced by her. A woman of great international fame in her life time, she had become almost a legend when she died at the age of 84. So much did she labor and achieve in the course of 65 years of continuous activity for her Jewish people, and so much goodness exhaled from her—it was hard to believe that it all came from a frail looking little woman who was not particularly attractive in appearance, but whose face yet shone with an innate grace and beauty through the rare and mighty spirit which animated her.

I consider Henrietta Szold the noblest and most gifted woman to have come from American Jewry. She occupies a prominent place alongside such celebrities as Rebeccah Gratz, Penina Moise, Emma Lazarus and Rebeccah Kohut —indeed she tops them all. Her success as a leader and servant of her people takes in a whole gamut of activities covering a variety of fields of public usefulness. She was a teacher in the public schools of her native city of Baltimore where she also taught English to the Jewish immigrants who began flocking to America after the first anti-Jewish pogroms in Russia in 1881; she performed pioneer work in American Jewish literature as secretary of the Jewish Publication Society where she edited many of its publications and brought out into the sunshine of fame not a few of our prominent writers; she was most active in Zionist leadership and herself went to Palestine where, perhaps more than any one else, she contributed to the rebirth of the Jewish nation on its ancestral soil; and she founded the Hadassah with its noble humanitarian work which is her greatest monument. From Baltimore, where she was born in 1860, to Jerusalem where she died in 1944, her life was crammed full of labors for her people and she belongs to the comparatively small category of human beings to whom it is granted to live life to its fullest without the least loss of time, and to be of help and usefulness to the largest possible number. Such persons, as a rule, find their greatest bliss in their work and achievements, and Henrietta Szold was no exception. Especially was this true of her in the last thirty years of her life which she spent in her happiest labors in Palestine.

To understand the phenomenon of Henrietta Szold, one must consider the background of her life and up-bringing. Unquestionably, much of her character came to her by way of inheritance from her parents and through the stimulus of a happy and idyllic home life. She was the daughter of Rabbi Benjamin Szold and his good wife, Sophie. Both Dr. and Mrs. Szold were of Hungarian origin and both were steeped in German culture which predominated in Europe in the first half of the 19th century. Rabbi Szold received his rabbinical training in Germany and was in his day regarded as an outstanding scholar among the rabbis. This meant much a hundred years ago when the terms rabbi and scholar were synonymous—unlike the situation in our own age when the rabbinical calling has become a highly specialised field in which Biblical or Talmudical scholarship plays a minor part. Rabbi Szold rose above the average in his sacred profession. He became noted for his Biblical research work, and his book on Job, published in the United States, which he wrote in a classical Hebrew, is among the notable contributions to Bible studies made in this country. But Dr. Szold was more than a scholar. He took his rabbinical duties very seriously, was a teacher, counsellor and guide to his people, and his home was always open to all who sought his help and advice. Yet though constantly occupied with his rabbinical affairs and scholarly pursuits, he still found time for the outdoors and for gardening. Both he and his wife brought a love for the soil from their rural Hungarian home. Rebeccah Kohut, herself a Baltimorean of Hungarian Jewish stock and a close friend of the Szolds, relates, in an article she wrote about Henrietta, that in the rear of their home they had a large garden with the cultivation of which the entire family occupied itself. In summer time Rabbi Szold was in the habit of rising at about 5 A.M. for his garden work, and among the trees he planted were a vine and a fig tree—a reminder of pristine Jewish life in Palestine. . .

Mrs. Szold, too, was a most sympathetic woman to whom Henrietta, the eldest of the five Szold daughters, was greatly attached. I remember Sophie Szold well from my visit to Henrietta in her New York apartment in 1909. Dr. Szold had already been dead about seven years, and though all the other children would have been happy to have the mother live with them, Mrs. Szold preferred to live with Henrietta. My visit there that year was shortly after Henrietta's return from her first visit to Palestine, on which her mother accompanied her. In Baltimore Sophie Szold was noted for her hospitality and for her skill in baking, cooking and embroidery. She made an ideal helpmeet to her eminent husband.

A highly interesting trait in Rabbi Szold's character was his ardent love of liberty which, no doubt, had much to do with his leaving Europe for America. In his youth this spiritual teacher and man of peace was a fiery revolutionary who, in the uprisings for the cause of democracy in Europe in 1848, was among those who fought at the barricades in Vienna where he was then a student. He retained this combative spirit for liberty after he settled in the United States where he became rabbi of the largest congregation of Baltimore of those days. Upon the outbreak of the Civil War Baltimore became noted for its sympathy for the South, and the Jews of the city, too, were on the side of the Confederacy. But Rabbi Szold courageously espoused the cause of the emancipation of the Negroes, and for this stand gained for himself not a few critics and foes among the members of his congregation.

Such was the atmosphere in which our Henrietta grew up, one of reverence for Jewish traditions and of intense love for the Jewish people. Her father's great erudition had a marked influence upon her spiritual development. Had she, the eldest, been born a male her father, doubtless, would have wished his first-born to follow him in the rabbinical calling, in keeping with the best tradition of the rabbinate. Not having any sons the good Doctor was anxious to see his daughter at least a Jewishly-learned woman, and in this he was quite successful. For many years Henrietta devoted herself to the study of Hebrew, the Bible and the Talmud and she interested herself in the "science of Judaism" which was then making such great progress in Germany and Austria-Hungary. German was then the language of the Jewish intellectuals and was freely spoken in the Szold household. Her knowledge opened for Henrietta the doors to the rich literature that was being created by the German-Jewish savants, from Zunz down to Geiger, Graetz, Steinschneider, Lazarus and Steinthal. She herself revealed an inclination for literary work early in her life. When but 18 years of age she began writing a series of highly interesting articles for the *Jewish Messenger* of New York, then America's leading Jewish publication. While purporting to tell of Jewish life in her home city of Baltimore, these articles actually touched upon problems which were then paramount in American Jewish life, such as the immigration of the Russian Jews to the United States and the attitude of the German American Jews towards them. The latter she unsparingly condemned as betraying a lack of sympathy and understanding towards the unfortunate victims of the Czar. These articles which she signed with the pseudonym of "Shulamith" served her well as a preparatory school for the work she was to perform with such fine success in later years.

It is important, I believe, to dwell upon Henrietta Szold's literary achievements for the reason that they had become overshadowed by her Zionist and Hadassah activities in the last thirty years of her life, so that the public today hardly is aware of her important contribution in the field of Jewish letters. The terrible Jewish tragedy in Europe since the First World War, and the resultant upsurge of Jewish nationalism, so completely absorbed her thinking and feeling as to make her swerve from the sphere of literary creativity for which she was so admirably equipped. But we should ever gratefully remember her outstanding work as the editor and translator of Graetz's monumental history of the Jews, Lazarus's "Ethics of Judaism", Slousch's important work on "Modern Hebrew Literature", Darmstadter's work on the Talmud, and her compilation of the "Index" to Graetz's history which is a great achievement in itself. As secretary of the Jewish Publication Society for twenty-five years she virtually edited all of the books that came from the society's presses including the "American Jewish Year Book", thus making her one of the pioneer builders of Jewish culture in America.

Nevertheless, the real monument she reared to herself was in her work for Zionism, for the Hadassah, of which she was the founder, and for the "Youth Aliyah" through which she saved so many thousands of young Jewish lives from the inferno which Nazi Germany had become. One cannot imagine the growth and development of the great Jewish communities of Palestine without the work she so nobly and heroically performed. Were she a poetess and inclined to boasting, she could in all truth have said of herself, as did Deborah of old, that she was a "mother in Israel". She who had no children of her own had indeed become a mother to her people and as such was turned into a legend in her own life time.

How did this woman come to Zionism? The story of it constitutes an important chapter in itself. Henrietta Szold was drawn into the Zionist ideology before there was any such a thing as a "Zionist movement" and indeed before Zionism itself came into being, which means long before Theodore Herzl came upon the scene with his "Jewish State" idea. Chronologically, her Zionist activities date back to 1881 when the fierce anti-Jewish excesses in Russia drove so many thousands of the Czar's Jewish subjects to the shores of America as a vanguard of a mighty hegira, and at the same time started the "Hoveve Tzion" (Lovers of Zion) societies which ante-dated Herzl's political Zionism by some fifteen years. The migration of the Jews out of Russia might have been turned towards Palestine had that land, then under the domination of Turkey, been so conditioned as to receive a large number of settlers. America alone was so conditioned, but coming to the United States the immigrants brought with them their "love of Zion" and started their "Hoveve Tzion" groups in the large cities where they settled, including Baltimore which received a goodly number of them. Many of them, looking for work, found their way to the home of kindly disposed Rabbi Szold who, with his hospitable family, gave them a warm welcome and helped them in every possible way. Henrietta was greatly impressed by the culture and refinement of many of them, and especially by their Jewish knowledge and their warm sympathies towards all things Jewish. From them she received first-hand evidence of the depth and magnitude of the "Jewish Problem" which was plaguing Israel and the world as a whole, and it was through them that she came to see Palestine in the new perspective of a future "Land of Promise" for her people.

She began her career of aid to her people by founding a night school for the immigrants to teach them English, the first school of its kind in the United States. Its phenomenal success in Baltimore made other big cities with sizeable Jewish immigrant populations follow suit. It is easy enough to say that she "founded" the school. In reality it was a most difficult undertaking. There was need of money even under the most economic conditions under which the school was operated and despite the fact that Henrietta herself received no remuneration for her work and never thought of getting any. But there was rent to pay and desks and chairs to buy and teachers to engage, since the volunteer kind proved unreliable. In her letters she scores the well-to-do German Jews of her city for declining financial help to this enterprise. She attributes it to ignorance and vanity. "They remember", she writes on October 25, 1891, at the time the school was established, "that they themselves acquired the good things of life without night schools etc., and let others go likewise. They refuse to take into account altered conditions, economic and social". She touchingly describes how the immigrants seize upon the opportunity to learn English and to improve themselves generally, and how old men and women sit alongside younger people, tired and worn out though they are after a long day's hard work. She sees in them a wonderful human material to work with, something refreshing as compared with the smug and self-satisfied Jews of the older immigration who have made their pile and care for nothing else. "So far as I personally am concerned", she writes in that same letter, "I am my father's daughter. Prosperity has something vulgar and repugnant about it. I feel very much more drawn to these Russian Jews than to the others—a prejudice as vile, doubtless, as the contrary one. Nor do I mean only the suffering Russian Jews. I mean those, too, who are earning a competency. There is something ideal about them. Or has the suffering through which they have passed idealised them in my eyes?"

It was from among these idealistic immigrants that the first pre-Zionist group was formed in Baltimore, and Henrietta Szold was happy to join with her pupils in its establishment. It was called "Hevras Tzion" or "The Society of Zion", and together with Henrietta there came in another young Baltimorean who was later destined to play a most prominent role in Zionist history in America—Dr. Harry Friedenwald. This happened in 1893, three years before the world heard that a young Viennese journalist, called Dr. Theodore Herzl, had written a little book in which he advocated the crazy idea of a "Jewish State", for doing which some of his closest friends thought he should have his head examined . . . . Henrietta even then had been convinced that the Jews were a "sick people", sick for no fault of its own but because of the world's unreasoning malevolence and inhumanity. A people that is sick is in need of healing, and the thought of a cure for Israel's ills never forsook her. It was a prime motive for her founding of Hadassah which adopted as its motto *"Arukat Bath Ammi"* (the healing of the daughter of my people), from Jeremiah 8, 22.

However, many years were to pass before she was to become the most dynamic worker in the Zionist movement, and before she was to undertake the most important phase of her life's work in Hadassah. Those were the years when Zionism was still more of a theory than a reality, when they who later became its forceful leaders, like Julian W. Mack, Stephen S. Wise and Nathan Straus still kept themselves on the periphery of the movement. The unhappy reality of Jewish diaspora life was then not quite as poignantly tragic as it became with the outbreak of the First World War when Zionism was catapulted into the world as a life-and-death problem. There was much dreaming and debating, Shekels were sold sparingly and conventions were held at which some fine speeches were heard, but the movement as a whole was creeping at a snail's pace. Henrietta herself was greatly occupied with her literary work in the Publication Society. Wholly active in Zionism she became after her return from her first trip to Palestine to which I have already alluded. It was then that Zionism first entered upon its "American" phase of development. Influential American Jews then began to interest themselves in Palestine from a semi-philanthropic motive, through the work of the "Jewsh Agricultural Station" which the late and eminent Aaron Aronsohn, the discoverer of "Wild Wheat", had founded in Palestine. Miss Szold became the secretary of the American branch of this enterprise, and shortly thereafter, that same year, 1910, she became secretary of the Zionist Federation which was the precursor of the Zionist Organization of America of our day. Zionism then completely captivated her, and she resigned her post with the J. P. S. to devote her entire time to it. Due to her efforts the movement was reorganised, enabling it to grow into the mighty organization it is today. But this was only a prelude to her Hadassah work, on which she was to embark three years later.

The idea of Hadassah came to her as a result of her first visit to Palestine, when she and her mother visited the Girls' School at Jaffa the head of which was Dr. Nissan Touroff (now living in New York). On the way to the school the two women were horrified at the sight of the many children afflicted with the dread trachoma disease which blinded ever so many of them. Swarms of flies were nesting in the eyeholes of the hapless youngsters who were so resigned to it that they did not even take the trouble to drive them away. Upon entering the school however, a much more cheerful sight greeted them. The children in the various class rooms looked clean, wholesome and without a trace of eye-trouble. Upon inquiry Dr. Touroff explained to them that it was all very simple. A doctor regularly visited the school twice a week and a nurse was on the premises every school day, paying special attention to the children's eyes. It was this that gave Henrietta the idea of organising a nursing service for Palestine. Hadassah was born in 1912, on Purim, which accounts for the name (Queen Esther was also called Hadassah), at a meeting held in Temple Emanu-El, New York, and it was Professor Israel Friedlander who suggested the motto "the healing of the daughter of my people". What is today the largest Zionist wing began with but 36 members. Interesting is the fact that Henrietta's own Baltimore "Landsman", Dr. Harry Friedenwald, was to play an important part in implementing the Hadassah programme in its initial stages. Himself a distinguished eye-doctor, he went to Palestine for a study of the trachoma disease and the means of combatting it.

They began by organising a visiting nurses' service, the first nurses coming from the United States. It was followed by the establishment of a school for nurses, then a maternity hospital, and finally by the great network of healing institutions which made Henrietta Szold's work in Palestine such a blessing to Jews and Arabs alike. American Jews, headed by Nathan Straus, began to give more and more generously to these institutions. But this meant much and increasingly harder work for Henrietta. She travelled far and wide in the States, addressed gatherings large and small, attended conventions where she brought her healing message, and carried on her propaganda by the written as well as the spoken word. Hadassah in course of time became the nerve-center of the work which had to be done in Palestine. But the idea of "healing" for the Jewish people embraced the entire diaspora whence many hundreds of thousands of Jews were to flock to the ancient homeland in the decades following the issuance of the Balfour Declaration.

Henrietta works on indefatigably, contacts many wealthy and influential Jews, writes hundreds of letters to friends of the movement and also to foes whom she seeks to convert. In 1920 she undertakes her second journey to Palestine and she remains there as a permanent resident though she visits the States every few years, mainly in the interest of Hadassah. Palestine is now her permanent home until her death. There she experiences all the throes of Israel's new birth as a nation, the periodic bloody onslaughts of the Arabs, the malevolent rule of the British, and the thrill of seeing the Yishuv grow, as if by magic, numerically, economically and culturally, the rise of the Hebrew University on Mount Scopus, and the marvellous transformation of the Hebrew language, dead for all practical purposes these thousands of years, into a living, spoken language which she herself acquires and masters with surprising ease.

Jerusalem is now her home town, and there she labors as zealously and energetically as she did in New York, and she is a very, very happy woman. Her Baltimore dream of a half a century earlier has become a reality, and she herself made a most notable contribution to that reality. There came the tragic Hitler years when the Jewish community of Europe is largely uprooted, and millions of Jews are threatened with total extermination. The now aged Henrietta throws herself into the rescue work; with youthful alacrity she organizes the "Youth Aliyah" to save as many of the German Jewish youth as possible, and herself undertakes the unpleasant and not very safe journey to Germany where she intercedes with Nazi officials and thus saves thousands of precious young lives from the jaws of the beast.

Two pictures remain in my memory of this remarkable woman. One is her visit to my home in Brooklyn in 1913, when accompanied by another woman she came to enlist my help in organising the Brooklyn chapter of Hadassah—today one of the largest of its branches. It was a cold winter night and we all shivered as we left the warm house to go to my Temple, Shaare Zedek, where I had arranged a meeting for her. The second picture is of my last meeting with her, this time in Jerusalem in the summer of 1935, when I spent more than an hour in conversation with her in her office at the "Sochnut" (Jewish Agency) building. It was a hot July day, and Henrietta was already an old woman of 75. Yet she hardly showed the traces of her advancing years; her mentality was as alert and her voice as firm as in her younger years.

Neither the cold of Brooklyn nor the heat of Jerusalem could deter this woman from the course she had mapped out for herself in the long ago when, as a young school teacher, she had dedicated herself to the task of her people's rejuvenation. She will always remain a legend, the legend of the Baltimore-born woman who died in Jerusalem as a Matriarch, a "mother in Israel", fittingly taking her place alongside of Sarah, Rebeccah, Rachel and Leah.

Abraham Joseph Stybel

To ABRAHAM JOSEPH STYBEL belongs the distinction of being probably the greatest mycenas in the entire history of our people. Perhaps more than any other man it was he who made possible the remarkable growth of modern Hebrew literature which, as we know, has been a most important factor in the development of present day Hebraic culture in Palestine as in other parts of the world, and in no small measure also influenced the political situation in favor of the establishment of the State of Israel. The coming historian who will tell of the great epoch in which we are living, will have much to say about the heroism of the fighting men and women in Israel who, representing but a small community of some six hundred thousand Jews, prevailed against the armies of seven Arab nations comprising about 40 million people. But this unusual record of achievement was made possible by the educational and cultural spade-work performed by a large number of eminent writers, poets, novelists, essayists, historians, teachers and all other promoters of the Hebrew word. Among them Abraham Joseph Stybel will always occupy a foremost place of honor.

Because Hebrew literature meant so much to him, Stybel gave away a huge fortune, said to amount to more than a million dollars, to promote it. I am tempted to speak of this as a million dollars which a comparatively poor man gave for the ideal which stood so close to his heart. For Stybel was far from being a rich man if judged by American standards. Even for a rich man to give away a million dollars is not an every-day occurrence. Yet Stybel, who was born of poor

parents and in his youth had to struggle hard for a livelihood, gave this large sum when fortune smiled on him, and
he kept giving to his favorite cause even when his riches left
him.

In the eulogy, which I was privileged to deliver at his
funeral (in September, 1946), I spoke of him as a true dis-
ciple of his namesake, the first Abraham, of whom Scripture tells us that wherever he went he erected altars to God.
Abraham Stybel, too, erected altars to the ideal he cherished
most, wherever he went, in Moscow, Warsaw, Berlin, Tel-
Aviv, New York, where he organised branches of his publishing enterprises, establishing periodicals like *Hatekufah*
and *Miklat* devoted to literature at its best, and printing Hebrew books in tens of thousands of copies, comprising both
original works and translations from the world's classics. For
Stybel was not just a philanthropist who gave money away
out of the goodness of his heart. Being a practical business
man he sought to place Hebrew literature upon a self-paying
basis, not to make profit for himself but as a source of remuneration to the writers and to insure its permanency as a
going concern. He envisioned the possibilities of a Hebrew
literature based upon mass production in which are engaged
the leading Hebrew writers of the age, each of whom is receiving a liberal honorarium for his work and is thus encouraged to proceed with his creative labors. He thus gathered around him a veritable army of writers, among them
men like David Frischman, Saul Tchernichovsky, Eliezer
Steinman, J. D. Berkowitz, Nissan Touroff, D. Shimonowitz, Jacob Klatzkin, Jacob Fichman, etc. In addition to their
own works most of these noted literateurs busied themselves
with translations from other literatures, so that there is
hardly a work of importance in the English, French, German,
Russian and other languages which did not appear in its

Hebrew garb under the Stybel imprimatur. Altogether some seven hundred such works came out from the Stybel presses which were kept working in Poland, Palestine and America from the day Stybel started his publishing activities down to the day of his death in New York, in 1946.

He was indeed the great lover who to the end remained true to the mistress of his youth. The Hebrew language assumed for him an importance of greatest magnitude not only for the future of the Jewish people as a national entity, but for its own sake, as the imperishable heritage of Israel. Was not the Bible—greatest of all books—written in it, and large portions of the Talmud, and a vast literature created by mediaeval poets, philosophers and mystics? And did not the golden chain of Hebrew letters continue through the ages and reveal itself in special beauty in the works of the Maskilim, the Enlightened ones, of the nineteenth and twentieth centuries? Stybel loved not only the sound of Hebrew, whether it be in Ashkenasic or Sephardic pronunciation, but the very appearance of the square letters, in which he saw a hidden mystic beauty. The tradition alive among the Jews that God Himself used the Hebrew as His vehicle when He created the world by saying "Let there be light", "Let there be a firmament", "Let the waters be gathered together", etc., was one that Stybel, though not a strictly observant Jew in matters of ritual, could well believe, for to him Hebrew was the one and only language fit for divine speech.

This love came to him early in life, while yet a boy attending the *Cheder* in his little native town of Zharky, in Poland. He tells in an autobiographical article that he was introduced to the *Cheder* when only three years old, and that his mother used to carry him there and back during his first years. The purely Hebraic atmosphere of that institution, and the fervent enthusiasm of his teachers for the Hebrew word as con-

tained in the *Siddur* (Prayer Book) and *Chumesh* (Pentateuch), left their roots in the child's emotional soul. As he
grew older Hebrew became more and more an integral part
of himself. Probably the very fascinating child tales of the
story of creation and of the Patriarchs, as contained in Genesis, had their effect upon him. Had he followed the beaten
track of going to a *Yeshiva* and studying the Talmud with a
view to becoming an Orthodox rabbi, it is likely that nothing
startling would have occurred in his life. As it happened,
his home atmosphere was too liberal for such a procedure.
Young Stybel's education did not take him far on the road of
rabbinic learning, but his knowledge of Hebrew remained,
plus his love and reverence for it.

He tells of the very first book of modern Hebrew that
came to his hands and influenced him throughout life. It
was David Frischman's translation of George Eliot's "Daniel
Deronda". By sheer accident his mother saw the book in a
neighboring town she was visiting and brought it as a gift
to her son. The story itself, with its preachment of a revived
nationalism for the Jewish people in Palestine, captivated
him, but he was fascinated even more by the beautiful Frischman style, which for elegance had no equal until then and
remains unique as such even today. Stybel read the book over
and over until he could recite parts of it by heart. It was the
first work he had ever read by a non-Jewish writer, and it
introduced him to a larger world. It was also the first time
he saw the name David Frischman in print. Many years
later, when Stybel was already established as a wealthy merchant in Moscow, it was this same Frischman whom he im-
ported from Warsaw at great expense to help him launch his
project of a ramified publishing enterprise, starting with
Hatekufah, a quarterly magazine. Frischman became his
mentor and counsellor, helping him lay out plans and find

the needed collaborators and assistants. The work called for huge sums of money, which Stybel was happy to supply.

I have before me, as I write this, the very first volume of *Hatekufah* which appeared in Moscow in 1918 in large folio size numbering nearly 700 pages. It contains the prospectus of the planned Stybel publications, and the vast scope of the projected plan is amazing. Tolstoy, Dostoyevsky, Pushkin, Tchekov, Lermontov and Tourgenieff of the Russian literature; Goethe and Heine of the German; Anatole France, Romaine Roland, Emile Zola, and Gustave Flaubert of the French; Charles Dickens and Oscar Wilde of the British; the Scandinavians Georg Brandes, Knut Hamsun and Henrik Ibsen; and many others, ancient and modern, are there. But that was only the beginning. Merely as an educator who brought the world's outstanding men of letters to the knowledge of millions of Jews living in out of the way places in Poland, Russia, Lithuania and Galicia, Stybel must be regarded as among the foremost benefactors of his people. The 33 huge volumes of *Hatekufah* some of them comprising more than 800 pages of folio size, in themselves make a tremendous contribution to our 20th century Hebrew literature.

As can be seen, Abraham Joseph Stybel was a man of unprecedented vision among our people. Israel Zangwill might have included him among his "Dreamers of the Ghetto". His vision was the Kingdom of the Spirit through the medium of the Hebrew language, and it came to him from his great pride in being a Jew. He, too, had the nationalist outlook— a Jewish State in Palestine as a solution of the "Jewish Problem". But if Israel is to become a nation once more, and if he is to endure as such, he must regain his own language, his old and beautiful Hebrew tongue, and in that language must come to life as great and noble a literature as any nation can possibly have. The translations from the classics of other peoples should serve as a stimulus for the Jew's own literary genius which, he was convinced, is as fertile and powerful in our day as it ever was. It was to bring this about that he devoted all his energies and all his genius as a moneymaker. This, too, is what made him unique among men. He who had the capacity for amassing wealth, actually had little personal use for wealth as such. He wanted it chiefly to make possible the grand literary renaissance of his people. As fast as he made money he devoted it to his Hebrew cause. And as I have already mentioned, even when things did not go well with him, he still kept supporting the publishing house he had called into being.

The story of Stybel's financial success is itself most interesting and worth telling. He was a petty trader in leather in Warsaw, when the idea struck him to build up a leather trade between Russia and the United States. Acting on this impulse, he addressed a letter to the Russian Ambassador in Washington. He wrote it in Hebrew, and, maybe, that was what attracted the Ambassador's attention. Anyway, he became interested in Stybel's project and furnished him with the needed information about the leather industry in the U.S.A. and its leaders, of whom he sent him a full list. Stybel wrote to each of the firms, but for lack of funds sent his letters without postage. They were received, however, and the young merchant was afforded the necessary credits and trading facilities. He was soon able to capitalise on his knowledge of the leather market. It also meant the laying of the foundation of a thriving leather trade in the United States itself. For years thereafter Stybel divided his time between Russia and America, so that New York and St. Louis became as familiar to him as Warsaw and Moscow. Came the First World War when the Russian army with its millions of soldiers needed huge supplies of boots and other articles, and Stybel got his share of the contracts. Almost overnight it made him a rich man, and as we have already seen, the money which kept flowing into his coffers went to redeem the vow of his youth to build up modern Hebrew literature to a position where it could proudly take its place alongside all other great literatures of the age.

Nothing else mattered to him, and nothing was permitted to interfere with his grandiose plans. Then came the Russian Revolution with its tremendous upheavals affecting the lives of 180 millions, among them six million Jews. The revolution found him in Moscow, where, as already told, he and David Frischman were working on the first volume of *Hatekufah*. The only effect it had was to delay by a few months the appearance of the work, so that instead of coming out in the fall of 1917 it did not appear until the following spring, for which the publisher makes due apology in a statement at the end of the 694-page volume. Bolshevist Russia—which later, under pressure from assimilated Jewish quarters, was to anathematise Hebrew as a "counter-revolutionary" language and banish to Siberia untold numbers of Hebrew writers, rabbis and teachers—at this stage was still deporting itself in a civilised manner and, at any rate, was too busy fighting the Black Hundred forces left over from the Czarist days, the Kolchaks, Denikins and Petluras.

Our A. J. Stybel made full use of his liberty of action for the furtherance of his cherished ideal. When finally he had to abandon his work in Russia, he moved to Warsaw where his publications began to appear on a large scale. From Warsaw he branched out to Berlin, Ţel-Aviv and New York, giving employment and incentive for creative writing to a large number of men who otherwise might have been lost to the nascent Hebrew literature. When World War II came with the Blitzkrieg invasion of Poland by the German hordes, Stybel found himself trapped in Warsaw. By the skin of their teeth he and his wife made their way out of the bombed and burning Polish capital and fled across the Roumanian border without money or even extra clothing. In Roumania he obtained funds he needed for the trans-Atlantic trip, and once safe in New York he was able to resume his business activity. There were a few lean years ahead of him, but in the midst of the struggle to reconstruct his life, Stybel, now aging and far from robust, never forgot his Hebrew ideal. No sooner was he in a position to do so than he began where he had left off, publishing books and resuming the publication of *Hatekufah,* the 31st volume of which appeared about half a year before his death.

Here, in America, too, he was animated by the same old ambition to make the Hebrew publishing business a living and thriving thing, and to work at it as conspicuously before the larger world as possible. He established his leather business offices in a prominent office building on State Street, in New York's picturesque Battery section. But on the huge window of his main office, facing the lovely harbor and the Statue of Liberty, was the word *Hatekufah* in large Hebrew characters, and it remains there to this day. Into this office streamed many of the leading Hebraists of the Metropolis, and his home, too, became the frequent gathering place of the elite of the Hebrew literary world. When he decided to resume publishing *Hatekufah* in New York, he did here what he had done in Moscow and in Warsaw when he began issuing the quarterly: he first gathered his literary family around him after entrusting the editorship of the periodical to two eminent writers. To secure the collaboration of the writers he wanted, he went to great lengths of persuasion, bombarded them with letters and telegrams, and, of course, offered them a tempting remuneration. I gratefully recall my own experience with him in this respect. He wanted me to write a series of essays on the great American patriots, statesmen and soldiers, under the caption of "Builders of the New World" (in Hebrew: "Bone Haolam Hechadash"). To make sure I would accept, he wrote and telegraphed more than once, had me meet him for luncheon to talk the matter over, and then sent me several books which he thought I could use for my work. When I turned in my first essay he telephoned to assure me that I had made him very happy, that he was very grateful, and urged that I continue to write. Several of his letters to me, bearing on his plans for the *Hatekufah* and on my share in the work, appeared in the volume of letters by Hebrew writers which I edited ("Igrot Sofrim Ivrim", Brooklyn, 1947, pp. 308-309).

Far from being a narrow-minded Jewish chauvinist, Stybel regarded the non-Jewish world in a most liberal light. He had many business connections with Gentiles and he and his wife were great favorites in Christian circles, both here and in Poland. But his interest in Hebrew never left him, whether at home or on a journey. Once when he and Mrs. Stybel were in Fond du Lac, Wisconsin, visiting at the home of Fred John Ruping, the latter told him about his Westphalian origin, his family's migration from Germany a century before, its settling in Wisconsin, etc. In producing some family heirlooms and documents, he happened to show him also the manuscript of a dramatic work which its author, a Dr. Karl de Haas, had left with Ruping's grandfather. The title, "Berenice", interested Mr. Stybel and glancing at the contents he saw that it dealt with the romance between that Jewish princess, sister of King Agrippa the Second, and Titus, conqueror of Judaea. He borrowed the work and spent that night reading it. So fascinated was he with it, both as a work of literary merit and because of its bearing on Jewish history, that he decided to have it translated into Hebrew, and the drama, in a splendid translation by Dr. Isaac Silberschlag, actually appeared in the spring of 1946. Thus did even his cordial intercourse with Christians serve to further his unflagging zeal for Hebrew letters. This book, incidentally, was also the last to be published by him.

Abraham Joseph Stybel at all times showed himself to be a complete Jew. There never was a question of a split in his soul between his Jewishness and his worldliness. His Jewish origin was not to him just an accident for which he had to apologise. The world simply had to accept him as the Jew that he was. To me he was a living demonstration of the powerful influence of the thoroughly Jewish training which was in vogue among the Jews of 60 and 70 years ago, through the medium of the *Cheder* and the *Yeshiva* in the numerous small towns of Poland, Lithuania, the Ukraine and Galicia. Bialik spoke of those old fashioned schools as the power-house in which was galvanised the soul of the Jew. In addition to the school there was also the home with its religious rites, ceremonies and festivities which exercised such an inescapable charm on the Jewish child. That influence never disappeared from the memory of those who came under it. In the case of A. J. Stybel it led to his becoming the mighty patron of his people's spiritual culture.

He was only sixty-one when death claimed him, and his funeral rites were attended by an enormous crowd, consisting mainly of the Jewish intellectuals of the Metropolis. And every year since his demise his death anniversary is marked by special services at his grave and by a gathering of his friends and admirers at his late home, where symposiums are held on his work and his unique contribution to Jewish culture. His friends are loath to part with him, and his presence is still felt in his apartment. It is a fitting way of commemorating the moral heritage of one of the truly potent spirits of our Jewish world. His wife, who has been such a true helpmeet to her husband, has continued his work and hopes to carry on in his spirit in years to come.

He definitely belongs to the category of unusual personalities whom a grateful Jewish people can never forget.

Sholem Schwarzbard

SHOLEM SCHWARZBARD was not a great man in the accepted, conventional sense. He wrote no books, not even newspaper articles (except in connection with his famous trial when he was sought out by the editor of a New York Yiddish newspaper and prevailed upon to dictate his memoirs and describe the events that led to his crime). Though well read, his education was mostly auto-didact. Nor did he ever lay claim to any measure of self-importance. He was a modest and retiring man, content to lose himself in the teeming crowds of Paris where he worked hard to earn his bread at his humble trade of watch-maker. Yet this little man, unprepossessing in any way, physically unattractive and with no ambition to emerge from the ranks of the lowly and obscure where fate had placed him—at one time occupied the front pages of the world's great newspapers, and in Jewish history will remain forever memorable among the distinguished champions of his people's dignity and honor.

He became that through—a murder he committed. In this, too, he was a paradoxical figure, and in himself adumbrated the new form Jewish life was taking as a result of the incessant persecutions and tribulations which plagued the Jews of the old continent with the rising tide of Antisemitism which followed the First World War.

That a self-confessed murderer should be acclaimed a hero by Jews is in itself a novel thing. It must not be forgotten that as a people Jews have ever shrunk from the thought of killing, even as a measure of self-defense. In all the bloody pogroms which took place in Russia in the reign of Czars Alexander iii and Nicholas ii, Jews showed themselves helpless to stand their ground, and hundreds of thousands preferred to leave for America rather than remain to fight it out. In the Kishineff massacre of 1903, when the Jews of that city permitted themselves to be slaughtered like lambs without putting up any kind of resistance, Chaim Nachman Bialik, the great poet, was thoroughly aroused over this supineness and wrote his immortal "B'Ir Ha-Harega" (In the City of Slaughter) in which he mercilessly chastised his people for not selling their lives and honor more dearly. Jewish history in Europe from that time on took on a new meaning. It meant that henceforth, if they were to survive, Jews must themselves become fighters, fighters and, howsoever repellent, even killers. In a world in which physical combat alone is permitted to settle things, one has to resort to it whether he likes it or not. Such, at any rate, became the prevailing thought of a large section of the younger elements of Jewry in Czarist Russia, which now proceeded to organise itself into self-defence battalions. In subsequent years and decades this philosophy was to assume a larger meaning, embracing the fate of the Jewish people not only of Russia but the world over, and its arena was extended from the Russian Jewish "Pale of Settlement" to include the whole of Europe. Ultimately, as we know, the combat was to be transferred to Palestine, leading to the Arab-Jewish conflict and to the establishment of the State of Israel.

Sholem Schwarzbard became a hero because he killed Petlura, the arch-enemy of his people who was personally responsible for the massacre of tens of thousands of Jews in the civil war which followed the overthrow of the Czar and the seizure of power by the Bolsheviki. Among those who thus dismally perished were not a few of Schwarzbard's own kin. These terrible happenings preyed upon his mind long after he settled in Paris where he fled from his native Ukraine. By a strange coincidence, Petlura, too, fled there after his bands were crushed by the victorious Bolsheviki. There, in the French capital, Schwarzbard ran across him, and the sight of the bloody Ataman brought back to his sensitive soul the nightmare of all the tragedies endured by his people in the land of his birth. No longer able to resist his impulse, he followed Petlura to his lodgings and there shot him as a demonstration that Jewish blood does not always go unavenged. The French jury before which he was tried readily realised that this was not an ordinary case of murder, and that Schwarzbard was far from being an ordinary criminal. It acquitted him, to the acclaim of liberty-loving people throughout the world (1926).

It was ten years after his acquittal that I, by the sheerest of accidents, met Schwarzbard. It happened in Geneva, in the summer of 1936, when I was there in attendance at the first session of the World Jewish Congress. A little later that same summer I again met him, this time in Paris through which I passed on my return trip to America. My first impression of him which I found no cause to change—was that of a man very simple in his tastes, humble, unassuming and unaggressive. He wanted but little for himself, was dominated by a sterling integrity, but at the same time was far from naive. Indeed, from our conversations I gathered that he knew life only too well, understood human nature, and was aware of the selfish motives which often drive men to corrupt, fraudulent and criminal actions. Against this he was always on his guard. He possessed a highly developed sense of justice and was intolerant towards any iniquity by whomsoever committed. I was also impressed with his inborn gentility. He refrained from making himself boresome in his conversation. He was a good listener and was careful not to interrupt when spoken to. But with all his modesty and simplicity he was quite proud both as a man and a Jew, and it was from this inborn sense of pride that stemmed his disappointment and chagrin at the world. Himself a socially-minded man, he was always concerned about the underprivileged and oppressed whose lot he wanted to see improved. He often spoke of the dawning of a new era of liberty and of decent human relations, which would also mean a final deliverance for his Jewish people.

We lived in the same hotel in Geneva and met daily at meal times, when we conversed freely about things of mutual interest. I soon learned that, unlike the great majority of men and women who had come to Geneva to the Congress, Schwarzbard was not a delegate, and represented no one but himself. He came out of his concern for the Jewish future which was so utterly threatened by the new wave of Antisemitism let loose by Hitler and his Nazis and wanted to see what the World Jewish Congress was going to do about it. But he also had a special motive for his trip: his interest in the affair David Frankfurter, the Jewish youth who, driven to exasperation by Nazi misdeeds toward the German Jews, slew Gustlof, Hitler's representative in Switzerland. Frankfurter's act of vengeance was so akin to his own against Petlura that he felt he ought to do something to help the unfortunate youth who was soon to be tried. He believed he could interest the representative Jews gathered in Geneva to raise the necessary funds for Frankfurter's defense. In this he was greatly disappointed. The notables who came to Geneva to take counsel on what to do about Antisemitism, showed little inclination to do anything for the man who, according to his lights, howsoever mistakenly, showed the way how to get rid of at least one Antisemite. . . .

Painfully disillusioned at this seeming indifference, Schwarzbard more than once mentioned to me his deeply felt disappointment. I wholly sympathised with him, for I, too, felt that Frankfurter should have received greater sympathy and help on the part of world Jewry. But there was nothing one could do about it. The situation created by Nazi Germany was of a most delicate nature, and if the Swiss authorities had to tread gingerly on the explosive ground, so had the Jews who had cause to fear that an open intervention in the case on their part, or even too great an interest in Frankfurter's fate, might make the situation within Germany even worse for the Jews there than it already was. The fact that the Jewish Congress leaders met in Switzerland, laid a special obligation on them not to do anything that might embarrass the country whose guests they were. Thus, with many others, I resigned myself to the inevitable, which later meant a long term of imprisonment for the young man. But Schwarzbard's repeated complaining, and the unmistakable signs of unhappiness he evinced made me take an ever greater interest in the man Schwarzbard himself. His deep interest in a man guilty of an act of murder so much like his own, made me feel that he presented an unusual case of psycho-analytical study. The great Freud might have found such a study of considerable profit to his science.

A small-statured man, extremely lean, Schwarzbard often behaved like a child, with all the attributes ascribable to children, their frolicsomeness, their savagery and their sensitivity. Like a young child, too, he was honest and incorruptible by nature. But unlike children who outgrow this primitive stage and become subject to environmental influences, Schwarzbard remained fixed in his infantile integrity. I still remember the ecstasy with which he greeted the beautiful sights of Geneva which he would point out to me in our walks

[195]

during periods of recess from Congress sessions, and his interesting comments on the historic places and statues in the public squares, on the Mont Blanc, most beautiful of all Alpine mountains, which one could see so distinctly from where we were, and the Lac Leman whose velvety waters sparkled so gaily in the inimitable Swiss sun-shine.

As we strolled side by side I would think of the psychological phase of this acquaintance with a strange and most interesting man, or rather of the effect of his companionship on my own psychology. For never for a moment could I forget that the man I was walking with had committed a terrible crime, had killed a man. By rearing and up-bringing, by all the moral codes I knew, by my professions as a Jew and American, I could never bring myself to make peace with the idea of private, self-imposed justice. To take the law into one's own hands, howsoever explainable by way of justification, is so remote from my concept of the civilised man! Yet here was this self-confessed slayer of a human being walking alongside of me, and his company was so agreeable and even refreshingly pleasant. The knowledge of what he did seemed to make no difference whatever. I felt not the least awkwardness or sense of guilt in being in the society of a man-killer; instead I had a sense of pride that my companion was of the select few who could well be described as a "hero in Israel". If I had any misgivings at first they were quickly dissipated by his softly spoken words and the vibrant and charming personality which they revealed.

I remember that Schwarzbard attracted my attention even before I knew who he was. Our acquaintance began in a most casual way. I was eating my lunch in the hotel restaurant when I overheard a conversation carried on by two men who sat at the adjoining table. The Yiddish they used had the flavor of the dialect as spoken by the Jews of the Ukraine, rich in expression but accented in a manner to suggest a rural Russian influence—unlike the Yiddish used by the Jews of Poland or Lithuania. The topic of their discussion interested me sufficiently to offer an opinion of my own, after stating my name and that I came from the United States. Schwarzbard somewhat reluctantly replied that his name was "Sholem", and I took that to be his family name. A little later, as we were sipping our coffee on the terrace, he bent over to whisper: "I am Sholem Schwarzbard. I did not want to mention it among all those people. You surely understand. . . ." It was then I noticed that his features were not strange to me, for I had often seen his pictures in the American newspapers during his trial. This modesty of behaviour revealed the man's character. He not only disliked publicity but feared and shunned it. He never sought to make capital out of the Petlura incident, and certainly was averse to being exploited by the curious and the sensation seekers.

And after Geneva came Paris where Schwarzbard brought me to his small but spotlessly clean apartment, where his good wife prepared for me one of the best meals I ever ate in that city of good eating. I was with Schwarzbard most of the three days I spent in the French capital, and I shall never forget his eagerness to make my stay a pleasant one. Together the three of us went promenading on the boulevards, visiting the Trocadero, the Eiffel Tower, the Luxembourg Gardens and the Louvre. He showed much pleasure in acting as my guide especially through the Louvre, where he revealed an amazing knowledge of history and of mythology in commenting on the various works of art. A professional connoisseur of sculpture and painting could not have done better, it seemed to me. With it all he never gave the impression of posing as an authority. His demeanor throughout was only that of a friendly companion trying to be of help and service.

His image haunted me long after I left him, and while on the return boat I often thought of him and even whiled away part of my time by writing an article about him which appeared in the "Jewish Spectator" of New York. I was searching for a key to the enigma he presented, that of a man of great refinement and utter integrity who yet could resort to murder to satisfy a grievance. It came to him, I concluded, from a highly sensitized nature and his great pride as a Jew. Schwarzbard's moral nature was like a precious musical instrument which under the touch of a genial maestro will emit enchanting sounds. Men like he, when they come across acts of wilful perversion and inhumanity, not only can shed hot tears of compassion for the hapless victims—they are also capable of working themselves into an ecstasy of revenge. Sholem Schwarzbard belonged to the category of human beings which gave mankind its heroic and sainted martyrs. Probably Mattathias, the Hasmonean, who slew the renegade Jew who sacrificed at the profaned altar at the bidding of Antiochus Epiphanes, or Judith, the slayer of Holofernus, were morally obsessed in the same way. When such men permit themselves to kill, they do so not out of sheer blind hatred but from a deeply-rooted sense of justice and of responsibility to society and to themselves. They take it upon themselves to act as scavengers, to do, what they are convinced, the constituted authorities had failed to do. We may condemn their act and at the same time must admire their moral courage, for it means self sacrifice for a cause they deem sacred. Their usefulness to society consists in the fact that they keep mankind's moral conscience from becoming dormant, or even altogether atrophied, by calling attention to existing evils and to the need of moral reforms so that life could be made safe and pleasant for the majority.

I heard from Schwarzbard in a letter he wrote me on January 7, 1937, when he acknowledged receiving the article I had written about him, and when he again took occasion to complain of the neglect of Frankfurter by the Jews. Some weeks later the newspapers reported his sudden and untimely passing at Capetown. With him went a great ethical and idealistic personality the like of which one meets but seldom among men.

Jacob Klatzkin

The death of jacob klatzkin, early in 1948, removed from Jewish life an unusually gifted personality, a noted writer, scholar and thinker. His going is a loss to the entire cultural world which, in our day, is so woefully poor in truly great men, men not afraid to do their own thinking and bold enough to hurl the truth, as they see it, in the teeth of a cynical world. But to us Jews his passing is especially deplorable, for we are a numerically small people and one suffering from a special weakness superinduced by the force of our being scattered all over the globe. Dr. Klatzkin was only 66 when death claimed him at his home in Switzerland.

To describe the merits and achievements of Jacob Klatzkin as fully as the subject requires would take me too far afield within the limited space of this essay. I would have to delve into Jewish life in Russia of sixty-seventy years ago with its heroic struggle for survival in the face of governmental oppression, and the inner friction between the "fathers and the sons", the older generation which was afraid of change and wanted to retain the status-quo of Jewish religious life within the frame-work of the Shulchan Aruch (the manual for daily religious living), and the new generation which saw its salvation in worldly culture and enlightenment. For the latter it meant a complete break with the past, a leap in the dark. Let me say here briefly that this struggle within Jewry has had a marked effect upon the course of Jewish history. To it we owe the new era in Jewish life which has culminated in the creation of the State of Israel. Like many others of the leading figures of his day, Jacob Klatzkin was a product of that period of storm and stress, and in the history of Zionist ideology he belongs with such outstanding men as Ahad Haam, Theodore Herzl and Max Nordau. That is to say, he was more of a theoretician than a builder, a diagnostician rather than a practical healer, yet his prescribed formula was essential if the patient was not to perish from the disease that was consuming him.

Basic to the Zionist philosophy is the idea of self-emancipation which was preached by all of the fathers of Jewish nationalism, from Hess and Pinsker down to Herzl. Jacob Klatzkin carried that principle into reality in his own life, when he completely changed himself from a small-town Ghetto youth into a distinguished European savant who at one time was the acknowledged literary mentor and cultural leader of the great Jewish community of Berlin. He came of a prominent rabbinical family which for many generations produced Orthodox rabbis and Talmudic scholars and authors. His father, Rabbi Eliyahu Klatzkin, was perhaps the most distinguished of his line and famed for his erudition throughout Russian Jewry. Young Klatzkin grew up in the patriarchal and strongly religious atmosphere of the little town of Maryampol, and under the zealous guidance of his sire had himself become imbued with Hebraic learning early in life. But the Haskalah penetrated even that out of the way townlet, and Klatzkin was captivated by it. He made his way to Germany, studied philosophy in the universities of Frankfurt and Marburg and subsequently in Berne, Switzerland. In due time the one time Yeshiva Bochur of Maryampol reveals himself as Doctor Jacob Klatzkin, the independent thinker and the author of many philosophical and biographical works in Hebrew and German, in both of which languages he acquired a masterly style.

It is my purpose here to dwell chiefly on Jacob Klatzkin

the man as I knew him in the course of many years, when there grew up a strong friendship between us. I got to know him intimately during the six war years which he spent in New York, where I would meet him every week either at his hotel room or at a restaurant for the midday meal. Our acquaintance, however, dates back to 1927 in Berlin, where I visited him at the office of the "Encyclopedia Judaica" of which he was editor-in-chief. That first meeting impressed me strongly and I remembered it for a long time. I saw him in action as Berlin's leading Jewish literateur, and knowing of his background and the transfiguration he had undergone, I could not but marvel at the man's adaptability and the skill and adroitness with which he carried on his affairs. He received me despite a very busy schedule, and again and again excused himself when the telephone rang or some of his collaborators came in to consult him about the work at hand. Callers of prominence were also there, and I remember meeting Deputy Isaac Gruenbaum of the Polish Sejm (now active in the political life of Israel), and the eminent Professor Ismar Elbogen. His desk was laden with manuscripts over which he was working when I came. Short and stocky, with a florid complexion, his smiling face exuded kindness and inner satisfaction. Here was a man who had conquered his own world.

But he did it at a price, and perhaps a very steep one. I was conscious of it while visiting with him and also after I left him. The price he paid for his transformation was the moorings which had held him safely anchored to a happy past and to all that went by the concept of home. I was already aware that he had married a Christian. True enough, his wife may or may not have become a convert, and I know that the marriage was performed according to prescribed Jewish custom, for he once showed me a "Kethubah" (marriage certificate) duly executed in Hebrew. But that was only a formality to satisfy the old Rabbi Eliyahu Klatzkin in remote Maryampol or in Jerusalem, whither he had gone to spend the last years of his life. Jacob Klatzkin was very fond of his father and quite proud of his Talmudic scholarship. From time to time he would pay him a visit, when he would let his beard grow so that the pious parent might be under the impression that his son was still an observant Orthodox Jew. He was very solicitous about the old man's feelings. But as far as he was personally concerned religion had long ceased to play any part in his life. His home was devoid of all Jewish rites and observances and the only child born of the marriage, a son, was permitted to grow up without any Jewish schooling worth mentioning. I met the son several times while visiting Jacob Klatzkin. He was a handsome youth who looked very neat and trim in his uniform as an officer of the U. S. Army. But he seemed more Teuton than Jew, and I often wonder how much he knew of his eminent father's writings. I felt certain that his sire's Hebrew works were sealed books to him.

Yet Jacob Klatzkin was a Jew of Jews all the same, and if he may be said to have lost the sense of safety and the moral anchorage that went with the religion of his fathers, he stood out all the more prominently as a champion of his people's rights, as a fearless defender of its traits, virtues and characteristics. Early in his career as a writer he won fame with his book, in German, on the problems of modern Jewry. It was there that he laid down the premise that there was no future for the Jew in the diaspora under the prevailing conditions and that the only hope for survival left for the Jew was in a State of his own—a thought which never left him throughout life, and he reverts to it repeatedly in his numerous essays. His scholarly work and philosophical dissertations, and more especially his devotion to Hebrew in which he cultivated a style of his own noted for its clearness and beauty, all stemmed from his love for his people and his desire to see it rejuvenated and rehabilitated as a nation in Palestine.

Coming back to my first visit in 1927, I was much impressed also with the trust and confidence which he, a foreigner and an "Ostjude" (Russian-Polish Jew) enjoyed among the native German Jews many of whom had been in the habit of looking askance at the East-European Jews who kept coming to their country. Dr. Klatzkin was a favorite among large circles of German Jewry, they admired his great intellect and were quite willing to help him financially in the grandiose schemes he promoted for the development of Jewish scholarship and literature in Germany. His "Encyclopedia Judaica" was a most ambitious project which required huge sums of money. It was to consist of fifteen large-sized volumes printed on the finest paper, with illustrations accompanying the articles which were to come from the pen of Jewish scholars from all over the globe. Ten such volumes actually appeared by the time Hitler came to power when Jewish cultural activity in the Reich came to an abrupt stop. The money for this as for other publications in both German and Hebrew came mostly from wealthy German Jews who appreciated Klatzkin's efforts as a worthy contribution to German Jewish culture and were glad to support them.

In New York Jacob Klatzkin, now a war refugee, saw himself in reduced circumstances, and I found him in a state of decline not only economically but spiritually as well. He occupied a little room in one of the cheaper hotels of Manhattan, and the seething cauldron of Jewish life in the greatest of Jewish communities barely evoked a ripple of interest in him. Not that the outside world forgot him altogether. He still had many callers, mostly friends and admirers from Berlin, who would drop in for a chat, among them noted artists, writers and dramatists. Their visits helped beguile the monotony of an otherwise lonely life. But he lost interest in all communal affairs and even in creative literary work. He would remain in his room all day, read the newspapers and listen to the radio. Invitations kept coming to him to attend meetings and dinners, but he seldom availed himself of them. Public celebrations ceased luring him. The worst of it was that he stopped writing, and if he accepted a call to contribute to a magazine it was not to write anything new but to give something he had on hand. He once showed me a drawerful of such articles, written in the lush-years of his literary fame but never published, essays on Jewish problems or philosophical themes. Some of them appeared in "Hadoar" or "Hatekufah".

Old age was creeping in on him, his health was poor, and he was alone. His wife was in Switzerland and his son in the American army. One thing he still retained, his old zest for life and what it had to offer. He was quite willing to stretch out his hand for the good things he could reach, provided it did not require too much exertion. He loved music and good food and often indulged in things the doctor had forbidden him. He found it hard to abstain. Summer time he would spend in Provincetown, Cape Cod. While in Boston several years ago I went out of my way to visit him in his summer retreat. I found him lying naked on the beach greatly tanned by the hot sun. He lived in a little apartment hard on the beach and evidently found much satisfaction in being away from all the exciting problems which agitated the world, and especially the Jews, during those war years. He sought to forget everything and just enjoy the present. Together we went in search of fresh eggs for the luncheon which he himself prepared.

Summing up Dr. Klatzkin's work as a writer and thinker, one must come to the conclusion that his main importance lies in his combativeness for the Jewish nationalist ideal. He is , of course, noted for his philosophical works. He wrote much to popularise the teachings of Spinoza whose "Ethics" he translated into Hebrew and of whom he wrote a highly readable biography. He also published a book, also in Hebrew, about his eminent teacher, Dr. Herman Cohen, of the University of Marburg. Klatzkin also did much to make possible the Hebrew renaissance, the revival of Hebrew as a modern tongue adaptable to all literary needs. Of special prominence is his four-volume Hebrew "Otzar", or as its Latin title is: "Thesaurus Philosophicus", which is based on the vocabulary to be found in the Hebrew literature of all times, beginning with the Bible, through the Middle Ages, down to our own day. It is a work of tremendous value. The poets, philosophers and Kabbalists of the various epochs in the long history of Jewry, particularly of the Middle Ages, which are so rich in terminology, all are made use of and brought into line for contributions to his work which is not merely a dictionary but also an anthology of philosophy, and contains the sources of the terms he gives. Had Klatzkin done nothing more than this one work, it should by itself suffice to insure for him a place of distinction in the hall of fame of our Hebraic culture. I have already alluded to the fine Hebrew style he wielded. In this he was largely influenced by Ahad Haam, though he went much further than his great master, and his diction is almost entirely free from all foreign-language traces and influences.

As a philosophical writer Klatzkin is not easy to read. His book "Shkiat Ha-Chayim" is a study of the human senses and of man's reaction to the phenomena of nature. It is a work which one has to labor through to get its full meaning. So, too, are many of his essays as published in Stybel's "Hatekufah" and in other publications. He was much more felicitous in his aphorisms in which he dwelt bitingly on human nature and its failings. An English translation of these essays under the title "In Praise of Wisdom" appeared in New York some two years before his death and deeply impressed the literary reviewers. He revealed himself there as a first-class analyst of human character and as such is first and foremost in our Hebrew literature.

His greatest eminence, however, as already stated, Klatzkin attained in the realm of Zionist ideology. Far from being a recluse as a student, he found his chief interest outside his ivory tower, which he repeatedly left for the busy marts of his people with whom he mingled and whose problems he never stopped studying and clarifying. And in the center of his thinking was Palestine as the one and only solution of these problems, the national homeland of the Jews and their political sovereignty as a State. Where Ahad Haam saw Palestine mainly as the Jews' cultural center, and where Theodore Herzl thought of the Jewish State in semi-philanthropic terms, as a necessary refuge for the unfortunate and persecuted, Klatzkin saw Palestine and Zionism as the sine qua non of the entire Jewish people. In brief, there seemed to him no future whatever for the Jews outside of Palestine. The diaspora life of the Jews he regarded as a losing battle against assimilation. To survive, spiritually and even economically, they must have a state of their own in their ancestral homeland.

He died about a year after he left the United States to

[208]

join his wife and son in Switzerland, but actually he died in exile, for his supreme desire was to settle in Palestine where he planned to engage in many cultural activities. His last letter to me, dated January 29, 1948, tells of his disappointment at not being able to carry out his plans because of his illness and the shooting war which had broken out between the Jews and the Arabs. His very last sentence there is an inquiry as to whether the "Hatekufah" is going to continue to exist. To the last his interest in Jewish culture and in modern Hebrew literature remained unflagging.

Judah Leib Magnes

THE LATE JUDAH LEIB MAGNES was a rare and enigmatic phenomenon in Jewish life. A native Californian (b. in San Francisco in 1877), he was in his ways more European than American. Certain it is that Europe had placed its indelible stamp on him in the two years he spent there after his graduation from the Hebrew Union College. It was from Europe that he brought back with him his interest in Zionism, in neo-Hebrew, in Yiddish. Traceable to the same European influences is also his idea of a "Kehillah" (a centrally organised community), on the order of the German-Jewish communities, as also his attempt to bring about a counter-Reformation in American Reform Judaism, to turn it into a "Liberal" type of Judaism as was in vogue in Germany, which actually was more conservative than the Reform practiced in the United States. Dr. Magnes possessed many splendid traits of character as a gentleman and a man of principle whom neither money nor personal glory could tempt away from what he believed was just and honorable. But he also had his shady characteristics which not a little beclouded his many virtues. In the course of this essay I shall dwell upon both the positive and negative sides of the character of the man whom I knew well and for whom I entertained a high esteem notwithstanding our disagreement on many questions of policy in Jewish communal life.

But first a few reminiscences about our relations in the fifty years of our acquaintance. They will, I believe, help unravel the enigma to some extent.

Magnes and I were contemporaneous students at the Hebrew Union College for two years, from 1898 to 1900. These were my first two years there and his last two, and in age he was my senior by about four years. The College, which today occupies five beautiful buildings in one of the finest residential sections of Cincinnati, in our day was housed in an unpretentious down-town structure which had been converted from a former private dwelling and as such had its shortcomings as a school. Nevertheless it endeared itself to us perhaps by the very fact of its small size and inadequate appointments. It was "home" to us, the students, where we mingled freely irrespective of our divisions as to grades and classes. As is natural in all such cases, we had our preferences in the companionships into which a student body automatically divides itself. We also had our rivalries and petty quarrels which, however, never led to enmity. The College kept us all united as one family, even as does a mother to her children.

As far as I can remember, Magnes at this stage was still unknown by the name of Judah Leib. It was either Julius L., or J. Leon Magnes. He was popular among the students not because of his affability, of which he showed little, but because of the great promise he gave as a preacher, and through his attractive personality. He was well built, a little over medium height, possessed refined manners, and his full, round face with its regular features bespoke self-confidence and a sense of self-importance. His professors were well pleased with his scholastic record, and all predicted a brilliant future in the rabbinate for him. I recall the sermon he delivered one wintry Friday night at the Plum Street Temple. He was well prepared, his diction was elegant, and there was a special appeal in his voice which captivated his audience. Old Rabbi Isaac Mayer Wise, who was on the pulpit and introduced him to the congregation, praised him highly for his effort and predicted that he would become a shining light in the Jewish ministry.

JUDAH LEIB MAGNES

Was it due to the laudations he received and the praises that were so often dinned into his ears that this young man became somewhat vain and uppish in his attitude towards the other students? As far as I could observe then he was rather fastidious in his choice of friends and companions. It may be that this state of mind had something to do with his decision to continue his studies abroad after graduation. He may have wanted to perfect himself through further study so he could rise in the rabbinical scale and be more than just an "ordinary" rabbi. Be that as it may, his decision to proceed to Germany for post-graduate work created something of a sensation among the students and served to raise him still higher in the esteem in which he was held. If I am not mistaken, he was the first Hebrew Union College man to do it—after him there were many others. We at the College followed with keen interest the news of his progress at the Berlin University and the "Hochschule", famous rabbinical school of the German capital, and when he returned to Cincinnati in 1902 with a Ph.D. diploma from Heidelberg, our admiration for him had no limit.

We soon found that the two years he spent abroad had made a new man of him, and perhaps even a new Jew. J. Leon Magnes came back as Judah Leib Magnes. He seemed completely changed in his nature, less finicky and more democratic towards others. The aura of a dominant self-esteem apparently had departed from him. He became an instructor at the College, and his great interest in the students and their problems made him a very favorite teacher. My own close relationship to him began at that time. It was my last year in the Seminary, and because of my special studies in neo-Hebrew and my work in "Haschiloah" Magnes sought me out and invited me to address his class on that subject. We became staunch friends. His signature is on my rabbini-

cal diploma among those of the other professors. Shortly after my graduation I received a call to the pulpit of Congregation Reim Ahuvim of Stockton, California, where I was
elected "unseen and unheard", and later I learned that Magnes, himself a Californian who had officiated in that pulpit
during the High Holydays, had used his influence in my
behalf. My parents in New York were not quite happy about
my "exiling" my self so far away to a place which then
took five days to reach by train. I remained there only a
year, but actually my stay was quite pleasant. The congregation was very small and my duties were few, and I availed
myself of my nearness to Berkeley to continue my post-graduate studies at the University there under Professor Max L.
Margolis, the noted Bible scholar. In this manner I spent two
days of each week.

With Magnes, who was still tutoring at the Hebrew Union
College, I corresponded during that year, and at his request
I occasionally visited his folks who were living in nearby
Oakland. I was very favorably impressed with the family
which consisted of the father, three daughters and another
son. Magnes' mother must have been dead then, for I do not
recall meeting her. They were of Polish-Jewish origin and
had originally settled in California probably as long ago as
a hundred years—as per the account given me by a second
cousin of J. L. Magnes now living in my city. With the arrival
of summer Magnes came to Oakland to spend his vacation
with his people, and one day he and Dr. Margolis surprised
me in my room on the Campus. I was then in the process of
raising a beard, and I recall the good-natured fun he poked
at my "Berdel".

Shortly thereafter I left Berkeley to return to New York,
and later that summer (1904) Magnes, too, arrived in the
Metropolis. He had resigned his position at the College to

[214]

become rabbi of Temple Israel of Brooklyn. We kept in touch with each other by mail, and one day I received a card from him telling me that he would pay me a visit at ten o'clock the next morning. When he arrived he told me that the object of his visit all the way from Brooklyn (they had no subway in those days and the trip was long and tedious) was to ask me for the last few numbers of "Haschiloah" which he believed I possessed. Such was the measure of his interest in neo-Hebrew literature in those days.

It is well to bear in mind the date of his arrival in Brooklyn, for with it began a new chapter in the history of the rabbinate of the great Metropolis. Temple Israel of Brooklyn was then a small building with a congregation quite limited in number, but it soon became a center of attraction for the Jews of that Borough and for those from nearby places. The young and eloquent rabbi was gaining fame rapidly with his earnest and warm-hearted appeal to the finer Jewish emotions as well as to the intellect of his people. He was a new and Prophetic voice, and in him the Jews of the rapidly growing community on both sides of the East River discovered a spiritual leader of rare qualities. In Reform Judaism Judah L. Magnes introduced a new line of religious thinking. He not only preached glowingly but demanded a radical change from the old rut into dynamic religious activity, not merely attendance at services in the Temple but a restoration of rites and ceremonies at home. He also asked for a closer relationship and a better understanding between the richer "Up Town" Jews and their humbler immigrant brethren who were the denizens of the dingy "Down Town" districts. Forty-five years ago there was still a gulf separating the two sections of the Metropolitan Jewish community, and Magnes attempted to bridge it. Unity within Israel was his ardent ideal on which he harped again and again. He thus became the outstanding rabbinical figure of New York of those days. Later another such figure appeared in Stephen S. Wise, but at the time I speak of, 1904, Wise was still in Portland, Oregon. It need not have been a surprise therefore, that after serving but a short time (about two years) in the small Brooklyn Temple he should have been chosen as rabbi of the largest and wealthiest congregation of Manhattan, Temple Emanu-El, where he was to minister together with its senior rabbi, Dr. Joseph Silverman.

As it turned out, what should have been the high-water mark of his success actually denoted the beginning of his professional decline. No other young rabbi ever faced such a rare opportunity for service to his people in a congregation that needed and wanted it as did Temple Emanu-El of New York at the time Magnes was called to its pulpit. It was an unusual honor for a man so young to serve in that congregation which then, perhaps even more than now, numbered among its membership some of the most distinguished Jews of America, men like Louis Marshall, Jacob H. Schiff, the Ochses, the Sulzbergers, the Gottheils and numerous others famous for their devotion to Judaism and to their people's cause the world over. But by the same token, no other rabbi occupying the heights of his sacred calling so willfully threw away his chance in the Jewish ministry as did Dr. Judah L. Magnes.

What happened was something with which a skilled psychiatrist might profitably have occupied himself. For Magnes was at first a highly sensational success in Emanu-El. The crowds flocked to hear him, the press had its reporters to take down his sermons, and he was lionised on all sides as New York's most gifted Jewish preacher. But it was this very phenomenal success which led to his downfall. As I see it, Magnes was psychologically incapable of standing up to success, where he would assuredly have stood up to failure and come out all the stronger for the ordeal. The very incense that was burnt in his nostrils made him dizzy, and once again there appeared a trace of his one-time snobbishness of Hebrew Union College days which we all believed he had rid himself of while in Europe. Was it also the result of the fact that by now he had become economically independent through a rich marriage he had contracted? None can answer this, and it is part of the enigma.

Far better would it have been for the cause of American Judaism, and of the rabbinate, had Judah L. Magnes remained a mediocre rabbinical success, content to serve his people in a provincial community where the spiritual rewards would have compensated him for all the other emoluments that go with a big-city pulpit. For Magnes had much to give to his people in spiritual terms, not only as a preacher but as a scholar, thinker and writer. Apart from his wide culture he also had a richly endowed nature, was a man of ideals and of poetic and prophetic vision. In New York these gifts of his were largely wasted. At the bottom of it all, it seems to me, was his belief in himself, his obsession that he was a great man. This was evidenced years later by his refusal to accept an honorary doctorate from a well-known American institution of learning, thus giving the impression that he felt himself above all such earthly honors. It was this Messiah-complex which kept him apart from his rabbinical brethren, their meetings and conferences. Outstanding a man as he was by virtue of his many accomplishments, Magnes would indeed have proved himself a great man had he not been conscious of his greatness. The truly great, from Hillel down to Einstein, are always among the meekest of men. Of Moses, one of the few greatest in history, Scripture states that he was totally unaware of his greatness, for he was "very humble, more so than all the men that were upon the face of the earth" (Numbers 12, 3).

This mentality, stemming from an egotistical complex, was to determine Magnes' entire future life. It affected, first of all, his work as a rabbi. In the pulpit he was now more than ever a prophet of wrath and of doom to his people whom he took severely to task for their un-Jewish lives, their religion-less homes, and the inter-marriage of their children. It all made interesting and sensational newspaper headlines but after a while became somewhat monotonous both to his congregation and to the general public, and ultimately had the very opposite effect from what was intended. It irritated where it should have stimulated. Magnes failed to realise that important as is the work of the rabbi in the pulpit, it is even more important that he be a counsellor and guide to his people through an educational process patiently conducted, and by means of personal contact. His temperament and sense of self-importance made him keep aloof from his members, to talk down to them from the heights instead of, Moses-like, coming down to them in the valley. Trouble began to brew which before long was to lead to catastrophe and soon the New York press carried the announcement that Dr. Magnes had resigned from his post. Altogether he served in that distinguished pulpit not more than four years.

It was a tragic occurrence, not because of the loss to him of so eminent a post as because it meant eventually the loss of Magnes himself to the rabbinate for which he was so well fitted and where, under different circumstances, he might have rendered such great service. After Emanu-El, it was difficult for him to find a suitable pulpit. Justice requires that I state that Dr. Magnes did not immediately abandon his hopes of serving his people as a rabbi. Indeed he held on to his rabbinical work for several years longer, accepted a pulpit in a New York Conservative congregation, where he remained a short time, and served for a few years as head of the Society for the Advancement of Judaism. But the day was not far off when Magnes and the rabbinical calling were to part company for good.

His experience in New York cast its long shadow over what was in store for him in the years that followed and notably in his work in Palestine where, impelled by his Zionist idealism, he went to settle with his family in the early twenties. A great work was awaiting him in the land of his hopes and dreams. The plans for the Hebrew University were maturing, and it was logical that he, the American-born rabbi with a Heidelberg Ph.D. degree and excellent connections with prominent men in his native land, should be thought of as head of what was to become a great seat of learning, probably the most important institution of its kind in the entire Middle East. Unfortunately for him, and not a little for the University itself, Magnes brought into his new field of endeavor the same mentality and the same sense of self-esteem which had proven so disastrous to him in New York. Not content with the urgent and pressing work of building up the University—and he did indeed succeed in obtaining large sums for it from American Jews in addition to developing its curricula and teaching staffs—he launched out on political activities which soon made him the stormy petrel of the Yishuv, where he organised the "Brith Shalom" and later the "Ichud" party which aimed at making Palestine into a binational, Arab-Jewish state. It mattered little to him that the great majority of his people, both in and out of Palestine, were against his plans, and that the very Arabs whom he sought to conciliate refused to grasp the hand of peace and friendship he held out to them. So self-righteous was he in his own eyes that the attacks levelled at him on all sides for being out of step with the vast bulk of the Jews, failed to make any impression on him, and he occupied himself with his political work, which was universally condemned, down to the last day of his life.

It is a sad summing up of a most interesting and nobly intentioned life, but truth compels one to say that, spiritually speaking, his was a life noted for its failures rather than its successes. He failed in pretty nearly every thing he undertook as a rabbi, as a Zionist, as an organiser of the "Kehillah", as a promoter of Jewish unity which was his dearly-cherished ideal from his younger years. He who in his Hebrew Union College days had held out such a glittering promise actually attained none of the things predicted for him. The gifted preacher left no printed sermons to edify his readers; the scholar with such a fine record at college and university, never wrote a book that would attest to his scholarship; the man who stood in the center of Jewish life for almost half a century, never even cared to write his memoirs about the important people he met and associated with in America, Europe and Palestine during what proved to be the greatest epoch in Jewish history in 2000 years. Perhaps this last statement needs qualifying. Magnes did leave behind one little book of 96 pages, written in choice Hebrew, which I have before me as I write these lines. It is called "Bimvukhat Ha-Zman" (In Perplexing Times) and is a curious mixture of a few addresses he delivered during the war years at the opening sessions of the Hebrew University together with eulogies of his deceased friends Aaron Aronsohn, Max Schlesinger and Henrietta Szold. We should be thankful for even this legacy for it reveals in a measure his sympathetic attitude towards people whose friendship he relished. At the same time it only proves how much more he might have done for the enrichment of our Hebrew literature had he but taken the time and the pains to write.

And yet, notwithstanding these blemishes in a man who tried so hard, though unsuccessfully, to be of service to the people he loved best and to Jewish causes he so ardently espoused one cannot but think of him gratefully for what he did for the Hebrew University to which he gave more than a quarter century of devoted service and which he helped raise from its infancy to the status of a great school of learning and research. No little recognition and appreciation is due him for the mere fact of his settling in Palestine and raising his family there at a time when the country was mostly waste and devoid of the many basic comforts and educational facilities Americans are accustomed to. It also required courage of a high order to remain there all these years in the face of the strife and the bloody clashes between the Jews and the Arabs. The University on top of Mount Scopus is a monument which will remind all coming generations of the highly gifted American rabbi who, after meeting defeat in his own country, found his greatest success in Palestine. Certainly his contemporaries who knew him well will think appreciatingly of his honest approach to life, his highly moral character and his firmness in matters of principle. Thus will the shadows which linger over his image be made to flee before the sunshine of his idealistic personality.

Stephen Samuel Wise

I ATTENDED STEPHEN S. WISE'S FUNERAL RITES at Carnegie Hall and saw the long lines of thousands of mourning men and women who flocked there and waited for hours in the hope of being able to get in. The police estimated that there were fifteen thousand or more in the crowd outside the building, in addition to the three thousand persons who were fortunate enough to find seats inside. I was among the latter, but even with my card of admission to the orchestra part of the hall, the thousands of us who were thus specially favored had to come early and wait long on the street, four abreast, before the doors were finally opened. The huge gathering on the side-walks represented Metropolitan New York as well as places far from and near the big city where for more than forty years Rabbi Wise labored zealously and courageously for the betterment of human life and, more especially, for the improvement of the lot of his own people. It was a conglomerate of peoples of different racial strains and of various religious faiths, Christians and Jews, Orthodox rabbis, Negroes, Chinese—all came to pay their respects to the man whom they revered so greatly, whom they regarded as their leader and teacher and as the champion of their rights as human beings. I doubt if New York had ever witnessed a like spontaneous demonstration at the death of a favorite son as it did in the case of this lamented chieftain.

As I sat through the hour-long ceremonial, listening to the music, the prayers, recitations and eulogies, it all seemed so unreal that Stephen Samuel Wise should be dead and in his coffin on the very platform from which for more than a

quarter century he had held forth, thundering out in eloquent
and impassioned words the truths he believed in. But was he
truly dead? His lifeless form did indeed lie there under a
blanket of white roses and amidst a profusion of wreaths of
all sorts of flowers, flanked by a guard of honor of Jewish
members of New York's Police Department. But actually he
was there himself fully alive and as if personally directing
the proceedings as had been his wont during the many years
and decades he preached there. It is known that he had himself arranged the programme of his obsequies shortly before
his passing and the entire service was executed in a manner
which would have met with his entire approval for its dignity, decorum and the Jewish motif it presented. It was indeed a Stephen S. Wise atmosphere, for the last time, alas,
in that place, though Carnegie Hall will be linked with his
name for a long time to come.

I believe that Carnegie Hall was a symbol of what Stephen
S. Wise was and stood for. It symbolised his vision as a
religious leader as well as his boundless energy as an organiser of the liberal forces of the community into a great and
mighty force for good. A man of his temperament and will
to serve and to achieve, could not be cramped into the four
walls of an ordinary synagogue, be it even a Temple Emanu-
El. By bringing his synagogue into Carnegie Hall, Wise demonstrated the true function of liberal religion—to bring religion's message into the very heart of a community as
surging and seething with life as is New York, and to do it
on the largest possible scale. And, of course, it meant to
serve the best interests of Jewry, to represent Judaism at its
noblest and finest. For, first and last, Stephen Wise was the
devout and enthusiastic Jew. I am sure that Wise purposely
held on to Carnegie Hall as the best sounding board for his
crusading views and ideas in the very center of life. He could

long ago have built his own synagogue had he so willed and tried. But the idea did not appeal to him until towards the last decade of his life when he knew that it was time to insure the continuity of his life's work in the "Free Synagogue" by giving it a permanent home for his successors to carry on.

He was a truly great man, and like all great men he had his failings and weaknesses which, however, paled into insignificance alongside his outstanding merits. At times he showed himself faulty in judgment about men and events. His opposition to Dr. Israel Friedlander's going to Palestine at the end of the First World War on a special United States Mission, was unjustified though to him his reasons must have been quite valid; it led to the tragedy of Friedlander's untimely death at the hands of bandits when, instead of Palestine, Friedlander went to the Ukraine to bring relief to the pogrommised Jews of that war-ridden country. I am sure no one regretted this unhappy development more than did Wise himself. He was wrong, too, when he spoke against the proposed boycott of German goods as American Jewry's reprisal measure against the Nazis during the height of Hitler's mad rule and anti-Jewish terror. He showed himself equally wrong, at times, in the stand he took on Zionist policies or rather politics. With it all no one could question the honesty of his motives in whatever he did, and no one ever gave himself more unstintingly to the service of his people than this man, who never rested from his labors, never looked for an easier road to travel when it concerned the welfare of the Jews, whose time was never his own but was filled from morning till evening with meetings and conferences, and who was always on the move, be it Europe, Palestine, Canada or the great Jewish centers in the United States when not engaged in preaching in his own community. In his day he was beyond a doubt the most sought after speaker throughout the length and breadth of America, and wherever he came he was met by overflow audiences of Christians as well as Jews. And he never disappointed them. He had the knack of bringing home his preachment in dramatic fashion, sweeping his audience off its feet when working himself up to a climax. In this he was helped not a little by his wonderful voice, a voice of rich timbre which he knew how to use to greatest effect.

Actually, though an integral and inseparable part of the big city on the Hudson, New York was to Stephen S. Wise only the spring-board for his activities elsewhere. I am convinced that to Christians he meant as much as any of their own great leaders when they looked to him for a message on the higher ethical levels. I recall his coming to Paterson many years ago to speak at a community Lenten service, under the combined auspices of the United Protestant churches of the city. The leaders of the Ministerial Association had asked me to use my association and friendship with him to invite him in their name and to induce him to come. When I told them they would have to raise a certain specified sum, not as compensation to Dr. Wise but for a cause he was interested in, they readily agreed. His address on that occasion was a history-making event in my community and was attended by perhaps the largest number of Christians ever gathered on such occasions.

Yet oddly enough, this eminent rabbi, though son of a prominent New York rabbi and scion of several generations of Hungarian rabbis, was himself largely an accident in the American rabbinate. By this I mean to say that Stephen S. Wise never actually studied for the rabbinical calling, and I surmise that the ministry was not among the original plans he or his father had for his future. He never thought of

[226]

going to the Jewish Theological Seminary which was already functioning in New York, his home city, and of which his father was one of the founders, or to the Hebrew Union College which was flourishing in Cincinnati and every year was sending forth its graduates to preach liberal Judaism in Reform congregations. It may be that his autobiography which, I am told, he has been engaged in writing in his last years, will, when published, throw light on this enigma of his failure to prepare for the rabbinate in the regular way, via a well-known seminary either here or in Europe. This does not mean to say that he was deficient in the necessary knowledge for the Jewish ministry when he did enter upon it. Indeed, Stephen S. Wise had excellent private tutors, including his father, Rabbi Aaron Wise, who ministered to Temple Rodeph Sholom in New York, Henry Gersoni, a highly proficient Hebraist, Dr. Alexander Kohut, distinguished Talmudical lexicographer, Max L. Margolis, noted Bible scholar, Joshua A. Joffe, Talmud professor at the Jewish Theological Seminary, and Professor R. J. H. Gottheil under whose tutelage he prepared for his doctorate at Columbia University. Had Wise chosen any other profession, he doubtless would have made his mark in it, too. Many believe that in him the American stage lost a great actor. By his build, his voice and his mode of speaking he would have climbed to the very heights of the histrionic art. Fortunately for the Jewish cause Stephen S. Wise did enter the ministry by becoming assistant to Rabbi Henry Jacobs of Congregation B'nai Jeshurun of New York. He was then barely 21 years of age (1893), which means that altogether he served his people as rabbi fully 56 years.

My first remembrance of Stephen Wise goes back to those years of his early ministry. He would frequently come down to the lower East Side where we then lived and to the Educational Alliance where he often spoke. I recall him as he looked then, tall, slim, stately, with side whiskers and a distinguished mien. I was a mere boy in my early teens and his occasional appearance at public gatherings in our neighborhood or at Cooper Union Hall, thrilled me and all of the vast throngs that would flock to hear him. Those last years of the 19th century presented a great and fateful epoch in the history of the world and of the Jewish people. There had as yet been no First World War, and the Spanish-American War still had to be fought. The "Zoological Antisemitism" which developed later was not even anticipated. Nineteenth century liberalism was still in the air, and we all felt that a better future was in the offing. True, there were six million Jews in Russia suffering under a heavy despotism, but somehow we felt that Czarism would soon be a thing of the past, what with the Russian Nihilistic underground assassinating Czars and making life intolerable for the tyrant officialdom, and what with the sweep of liberal thought which surely would before long include Russia as it did all the rest of Europe. Then there dawned the golden days of the Zionist dream, when Theodore Herzl electrified the Jewish world with his vision of a "Jewish State", to which the Jewish quarter of New York reacted with such marked fervor, its enthusiasm spilling over and embracing the more sedate and phlegmatic "Yahudim" (Jews of German extraction), so that they, too, became inoculated with the new virus, and their leaders would come down into the "Ghetto" and join with their humbler brothers in the new ideology. Foremost among these pioneer Zionists were the two Gottheils, Dr. Gustav Gottheil, rabbi of Temple Emanu-El, and his son, Professor Richard Gottheil, and along with them, as a most active worker for the Zionist cause, came Stephen S. Wise.

Zionism was among Stephen Wise's early loves as a rabbi and communal worker. It remained his one great love to the last.

If Stephen Wise did not learn his rabbinical craft in a regular Seminary, he acquired it while serving his apprenticeship in New York. The rabbinical calling is a most complicated and delicate affair. It has to do with the art of handling people more than with theology or even preaching sermons. B'nai Jeshurun congregation of New York was a splendid preparatory school for the young rabbi and there he won his first spurs in Jewish leadership. It was well that it was only the opening stage of his rabbinical career. New York was indeed where the gifted young preacher belonged, but he first had to pass through another preparatory stage out West, away from the maddening crowds of the great Metropolis and in a more completely American environment. Wise went to Portland, Oregon, where he stayed for a number of years as rabbi of Temple Beth Israel, an ultra-Reform congregation. In that Western atmosphere he completed his preparation for the great work he was destined to do in New York. The fame of Rabbi Wise had by now spread all over the country and got to Temple Emanu-El, where they were looking for a rabbi to minister alongside of Dr. Joseph Silverman. Wise was invited to preach, was offered the position, and he declined. This was the turning point in his life as a rabbi. If it was a great honor for a young man to be called to so prominent a pulpit, it was a still greater distinction for him to be able to tell that proud institution with its prominent members and Board of Directors that he did not want them and would not have their glittering offer. Overnight it established Stephen S. Wise in the hearts of liberal Jews everywhere as a champion of liberty of speech in the pulpit. It made a hero out of him in the eyes of rabbis and laymen alike. It also put ideas into his head about "invading" New York on his own and setting up his own bailiwick, which he did shortly thereafter.

Perhaps something should be said here about this episode. Personally I think too much was made of the entire incident, and the Temple Emanu-El Board had the greater share of the blame. The Emanu-El Board was anxious to secure Stephen Wise for its pulpit, knowing what an ornament and asset he would be. At the same time it must have had misgivings about the fiery temperament of the young preacher and the uses he was likely to make of his opportunities in New York. If restrictions were suggested on the rabbi's pulpit work it was surely done from a sense of responsibility towards the community and not out of lack of a proper respect for the dignity of the pulpit or even for the freedom of speech of the rabbi. I do not think Temple Emanu-El ever restricted the freedom of speech of any of its rabbis. It surely did not require its rabbis, among whom had been distinguished men like Samuel Adler and Gustav Gottheil, to submit to the humiliating procedure of having their sermons censored by the Board. The same holds true of any congregation in America. In all of the 43 years that I have functioned as rabbi in several congregations, I have not once been asked to submit a sermon for scrutiny and approval before its delivery. It did happen once that the president of my congregation asked me not to speak on the subject I had announced in my Temple Bulletin and the newspapers—he was afraid it might prove controversial. I promptly turned down his request, preached my sermon as planned, and had extracts of it printed in the next day's papers. I am sure that rabbis all over the country can attest to the complete freedom of utterance they enjoy in their preachments, though some of them, sometimes, get into difficulties *after* preaching—which is perhaps as it should be. Temple Emanu-El of New York was no different in this respect from the rest of Reform Jewry in America.

Even so, let me say, it was rather rash on the part of the Board of Trustees of that noted congregation to even hint at such restrictions. They should have known that a man who is fit and worthy of the exalted position of rabbi should be trusted to use his right judgment in what he says; should, in other words, be thrown upon his own responsibility to his people and his conscience. And, anyway, they should have known that, of all men, Stephen S. Wise would be the last to accept any form of restraint; that he would even make an issue of it to their detriment. This is exactly what happened. Wise seized upon this occasion to proclaim the sacred and inviolable principle of pulpit freedom, and used it as a lever for the realization of his long-cherished hopes of establishing himself in New York. He might have done this, and successfully, even without all the fanfare of publicity which followed the Emanu-El controversy, for by now he had become a past-master in the art of organiser. But the Emanu-El incident supplied him with a short-cut to his phenomenally successful career in New York.

I have before me a letter I received from Wise at the time this controversy was raging in our Jewish world—in answer to one I had written him. It is dated Portland, Ore., January 27, 1906, and is, I believe, well worth quoting in full:

"My Dear Raisin:

Let me thank you for your words of January 22, in which you express your agreement with my position in the matter of the call, which it was the purpose of the Trustees of Temple Emanu-El to extend

to me. As you understand, there was nothing else
for a self-respecting Rabbi to do. However much it
may now be sought to evade or to becloud the issue,
it was deliberately attempted by Mr. Marshall and his
colleagues who are under his domination, to muz-
zle and throttle their pulpit. I need not tell you that
it is not true that I threatened to preach politics, for
I never have preached politics in any pulpit which
I have occupied, unless to speak out on civic shame
be to preach politics.

I am the more appreciative of your word because,—you will hardly believe this—you are one
of less than half a dozen men in the Jewish ministry in the United States, from whom I have heard
since the appearance of my open letter. Think of
the pity and shame of it—not a single Rabbi in New
York has spoken a word. The complacency with
which the men, who occupy the pulpits of the larger
congregations, wear their muzzles, is to me unspeak-
ably sad. I mean to continue the fight, even though
I should stand alone, and yet such men as you make
me feel that I do not stand alone and that I have
brothers in the ministry who, with me, mean to free
the pulpit.

Possibly you have heard that I have decided to
leave Portland within the next few months, in order
to organise and lead an independent Jewish religious movement in New York. I mean, by that, a
free Synagogue, with a free pulpit, standing for a
free, vital and progressive Judaism.

With cordial greetings, I am,

Sincerely yours,

Stephen S. Wise".

The letter is quoted exactly as he wrote it, with his spelling and orthography, and his underscoring.

Whether or not he was fully correct in the interpretation he placed upon that incident, I think it was all to the good as far as the results were concerned. The "Free Synagogue" which he fathered and nurtured has become a powerful influence for better and happier living in the more than 40 years of its existence; and it added considerable glamour and picturesqueness to the life of the Metropolis. In Stephen Wise's hands it served as a mighty instrument for great social enterprises. Wise was not content with mere preaching, but converted words into deeds. In addition to the usual congregational activities, like a religious school, a Sisterhood, a Brotherhood, he also established social welfare work in Bellevue Hospital, founded a child-adoption bureau in which his wife—herself a great and noble personality—considerably helped him, and performed invaluable services in the Congress Houses he called into being to shelter the hapless refugees from the Hitler horror. Out of the Free Synagogue emanated the forces that helped create the American Jewish Congress, the World Jewish Congress, and the Jewish Institute of Religion. Because of his eminent success in his Synagogue, Stephen S. Wise was able to play an even more notable part in the Zionist movement where to the last he remained a dominant and outstanding figure.

Stephen S. Wise was the great tribune of his people, the Jewish apostle to the Gentiles, a man truly and deeply human; he was always conscious of his own importance, but never so much as to forget the bonds that tied him to the world, even to the humblest and lowliest men. He was American Jewry's greatest contribution to world Jewry, as distinguished a figure abroad as he was in his own country. I

heard him speak to a vast congregation in the American
Church in Paris, and I attended the great reception given in
his honor at the King David Hotel in Jerusalem (1935). I
saw him at work at the Zionist Congresses, and at the World
Jewish Congress which he more than any one else, called into
being. Always a resplendent figure, he was in himself an institution of commanding power and influence, a teacher of
righteousness whose exhortations often assumed Prophetic
proportions, a warrior who was never afraid of a fight, and
never more eager than to accept a challenge for a worthy
cause. It is what explains his unusual popularity and affec-
tion among all groups and classes, as was reflected in the
remarkable demonstration given him at his funeral services.
It may take generations before the world will look upon the
like of him again.

Elisheva

AN ENIGMATIC AND A SEEMINGLY tragic figure was Mrs. Elisheva Bychovsky who died recently in Tiberias, Israel. She was famed as a Hebrew poetess and novelist, her pen-name, "Elisheva", being outstanding among the builders of modern Hebrew literature in Palestine. The enigma, and perhaps also the tragedy, lies in the fact that she was a Christian by birth who came to the old-new Jewish land from far-away Russia and adopted the Jewish people and religion, as well as the Hebrew language, as her own. For a full generation she lived in what is now Israel, laboring at her verses, novels and sketches, making a valuable contribution of her own to the new life that was evolving in the now resurrected land, and suffering great hardships in the process. I wish I could say that she relished the comforting sensation, the thrilling consciousness, of working and sacrificing for an ideal and for a people she loved and admired. Herein lies the great question mark. They called her "the Ruth from the Volga banks", but did this comparison to the idyllic Bible heroine fit our Elisheva Bychovsky? Did she, too, say in her heart on joining the Jewish people: "Whither thou goest, I will go; and where thou lodgest, I will lodge", etc.? The batch of letters I have from her, covering a period of more than twenty years, gives me reason to suspect that she was not fully happy in her new life. At any rate, it is a secret which she took with her to the grave.

Hers is a most unusual story, and beyond the shadow of a doubt she occupies a niche of honor in the hall of fame of new-born Israel. Her biography reads like one of the wonder-tales of modern times. Born Yelisavieta Zhirkova in Riazan, Russia, of a father who was of the Russian Orthodox faith and a mother who was English by descent, our heroine was brought up as a dutiful Christian in her native town and, later, in Moscow where she went to live with an aunt after the death of her mother. Early in life she showed signs of literary talent, and she made her debut in the Russian literature in 1919 with two volumes of verse which received the praise of the critics. Had she continued her work in her native tongue she unquestionably would have made her mark in the new Russia that was rising upon the ruins of the Czarist empire. But destiny led her towards the Jews and the new chapter in their history they were writing. Instead of remaining in the frozen steppes of Russia she wended her way towards warm and sunny Palestine where, together with her maiden name she also shed her Christian belief. Yelisavieta Zhirkova became Elisheva Bychovsky, wife of a Jew, Samuel Bychovsky, who was a Hebrew teacher in Moscow at the time she met him. Together they migrated to Palestine in the early twenties.

Before I delve into a study and analysis of this unusual character, I want to tell of what I knew about Elisheva from personal contact and observation. I first met her in Tel Aviv in 1925, on my first visit to Palestine. I had read her remarkable verses and essays in Stybel's "Hatekufah", and knowing her story as a proselyte I felt tempted by curiosity no less than by an ever present desire to meet the celebrities among the creative Hebrew writers, to seek her out on my arrival in that all-Jewish city. A description of my visit to her at that time I published, on my return to America, in the New York Hebrew weekly, "Hadoar". I found her in a little but spotlessly clean house in Grusenberg Street, not far from the beach. Before me stood a woman of about thirty, tall and slender, with a distinctly Slavic face. It was an extremely hot day and Elisheva was lightly attired and barefoot. Her little, one-year old girl, seated in a high chair, became frightened at the arrival of the stranger, and burst out crying. Her mother sought to quiet her in a few words—in Hebrew. I was impressed with her facile use of the language and the plain and clear enunciation of her words. She was working on some composition when I arrived, and among the books piled on her desk I noticed an open tome which she evidently consulted often. It was a Hebrew dictionary.

We conversed on a variety of topics, and I confess that her fluent use of the Hebrew made me envious of this "Goya", this outsider who invaded our cherished Hebraic culture and bid fair to become one of its pillars and high priests. Wasn't she an intruder? I had the sense of being beaten at my own game, I who had been a life-long student of Hebrew and who had to struggle hard to secure whatever humble place I attained in its literature. To this Gentile-born woman it seemingly came so incomparably easy! Even making every allowance for the advantage she enjoyed in living in the land where Hebrew had become a spoken tongue, her adroit use of it made me feel inferior in her presence. Before taking my leave, I asked her to pose before my camera, and she came out into the open with her still crying baby in her arms. It is one of my great regrets that, for whatever reason, the picture failed to materialise. It is a memento I would have greatly cherished.

This visit led to a correspondence between the two of us in which Elisheva's husband also participated. It developed that the economic situation of the Bychovskys was none too good, and was growing steadily worse. Samuel Bychovsky was not much of a provider, and his health was poor. Elisheva had to carry the burden of earning a living for the family, but Hebrew poetry paid poorly, and Hebrew novels hardly better. Besides, Palestine was fast becoming the mecca of men and women from Europe who worked at the same craft, including some who had made a name for themselves. The Hebrew daily press, now grown strong, absorbed a number of them, but Elisheva was not among them. She was too timid and shy to push herself and to set forth her claim to recognition and reward. The fact of her alien origin and conversion had long ceased to be a sensation. It would have been different, perhaps, had she remained a Christian and as such had come before the Jewish community with her Hebrew literary efforts. Having become Jewish herself, the glamour of her conversion soon faded, and she found herself exposed to a hard struggle for existence. Her letters and those of her husband which reached me from time to time, conveyed a grim tale of suffering, and I did what I could to alleviate their distress. I secured for them an annual subsidy from the Israel Matz Foundation of New York, and Elisheva found a part time position as a typist with one of the Jewish institutions of Tel Aviv. Her earnings from that source were small and it interfered with her literary work, which caused her much chagrin. In their letters both husband and wife asked that I help them undertake a lecture tour of Europe and the United States. Samuel Bychovsky was convinced that his wife's fame would attract large audiences, thus enabling them to raise the necessary funds to pay their debts and tide them over until Elisheva's new novel, on which she was at work, would appear and the sale of it, he was sure, would bolster up their shaky finances. I was unable to secure the money they needed and they never got to America, but they did go to Europe where Elisheva read lectures, recited her poetry and made little speeches in Hebrew before audiences in Warsaw and other Polish cities, but failed to make an impression. She had no talent for the stage or the speaker's platform and, shy as she was, the role of appearing as an "attraction" must have been a painful ordeal to her sensitive nature. They returned to Palestine poorer than when they left. Shortly thereafter the husband died, and Elisheva was left alone to care for herself and child as best she could.

I saw her several times since our very first meeting, in 1927 in Tel Aviv, in 1928 in Berlin where she and her husband stopped over on her lecture tour of Poland, and finally once again in Tel Aviv, in 1935, when she came to see me in my hotel accompanied by her daughter, now a young lady of eleven. The severe struggle she was up against had left its traces upon her. She looked tired and there was a note of discouragement in her words. One could easily see that she was an unhappy woman, and the impression I got from our last conversation was that her unhappiness was due not merely to her material poverty but also to the role she was forced to play as a member of the Jewish people. Her last letter to me, dated November 16, 1947, speaks more pointedly about her state of mind. "I am not a Jewess", she says in the course of her lengthy communication, "and just to make believe that I am one is something I cannot do". It is these words which make me feel Elisheva was a disillusioned woman and regarded her conversion as a mistake, a mistake tragic because irrevocable.

Such a discovery should make it all the more tempting for a writer to unravel the mystery in which the Elisheva case is shrouded. I believe that the key to the enigma should be sought in Moscow and in the turbulent events which attended the Bolshevik revolution at the time Elisheva appeared upon the scene as a Russian writer,—always taking into account her highly sensitive nature and the lofty idealism by which she was prompted. The overthrow of the Czar meant freedom to the six million Jews of the empire as it did to all the other oppressed minorities of that vast land. Jews played a most prominent part in that revolution, and not a few of them filled posts of importance in the newly established order. In many parts of Russia, however, notably in the Ukraine, a fierce civil war was raging, and among the victims of the struggle were hundreds of thousands of Jews. An echo of this conflict reached Moscow where a large number of Jews from various parts of the land had taken refuge. Many of them were divided in their attitude towards the upheaval and as to what it portended. The Zionists, whose number was not inconsiderable, regarded it as but another indication of the hopelessness of the Jewish position, and saw their only avenue of escape in migration to Palestine. As against these there were the assimilationists to whom Leon Trotzky, an alienated Jew who together with Nicholas Lenin had engineered the revolution, was a symbol of the new Russia with its possibilities of freedom and equality for all peoples and races. These renegade Jews became the super-patriots of the new order, were vociferous in their claims and demands, and pretended that they were the spokesmen for the entire Jewish community. Before long they were clothed with governmental authority which they used to oppress their own fellow-Jews. Known as the "Yevsektzia" (Jewish Section), the leaders of this group, to whom were entrusted all matters affecting the Jews, instituted a regime of inquisition and oppression which in many respects was worse than that of the Czars. While nominally enjoying equal civil rights with the rest of the population, Jews were forbidden to live as such religiously, to practice the tenets of their faith, to circumcise their children or to give them a Jewish education. At the bidding of the "Yevsektzia" many Jews turned

informers and man-hunters against their own brethren, caus-
ing untold thousands of rabbis, Hebrew teachers and Zionist
propagandists to be imprisoned and exiled to Siberia where
many of them perished and some are still languishing and
enduring what to them is a living death.

Elisheva was not Bolshevik enough to want to remain a
part of her own Russian people in the period of its revolutionary chaos and transition. Whatever her sympathies
towards the revolution may have been, she was not sufficiently fanatical or toughened to become a fighter at the barricades or behind the heavy guns. Yet when she became a
Jewess she did what was by far more revolutionary and irrevocable. She cut herself loose from her own stem, and that
was difficult and painful enough. But in seeking to graft
herself upon the Jewish tree she attempted what was well-
nigh impossible. For it was not, I am sure, a question of
religious conviction with her. Judaism as a religion did not
enter into the problem, save perhaps the sense that it cush-
ioned the shock of the transformation by the logic that, after
all, by embracing Judaism she was but returning to the foun-
tain-head of her native Christian faith. In and by itself, the
problem was one of racial and social adjustment, of un-
making the Russian in her and of remaking herself into a
Jew. From what I am able to gather from snatches of conversation I had with her and from our correspondence, it
was this which formed the core of a life-long struggle within
her and apparently remained an unsolved problem down
to the day of her death.

It is evident that Elisheva became part of a people whom
she did not really know or understand. She had been drawn
towards the Jews under the glamour of their great historic
importance, their brilliant gifts of mind and soul as demonstrated throughout their eventful history, their authorship

of the Bible, their cosmopolitanism and, last but far from least, their unequaled capacity for martyrdom in all the ages of which she was an eye-witness in her own day. In the internal struggle between the Zionist and the religious-minded Jews on the one hand and the "Yevsektzia" on the other, her inclinations were assuredly towards the former, and that was the determining factor in her decision to marry a Jew and to follow him to Palestine. But here she found herself face to face with a crude and unpleasant reality. The people she had so idealised often showed itself far from ideal. Fugitives from oppression and persecution, many of her newly acquired brethren often acted selfishly in the struggle for survival which they faced in their new homeland and in which, as in all such cases, the stronger took advantage of the weaker. Elisheva was too naive to stop to consider that such unpleasant phenomena are part of historic upheavals in the life of peoples and nations. She only knew that she was among the weak and helpless and that her own feeble strength made her a poor match against the ambitions of the strong and rapacious. She also must have been keenly disappointed at the lack of appreciation, as she saw it, of her literary attainments on the part of the people with whom she had thrown in her lot.

But I want to go a bit further in this analysis, for there is still another approach to the Elisheva enigma. I believe that Elisheva's keenest disillusionment lay not so much in the failure of the Jews of Palestine to appreciate her, as in the fact that she had become aware of her own incapacity alongside the great poetic luminaries who, like herself, had come to make their home in the ancient land and whose genius, of necessity, dominated and monopolised the scene, leaving all lesser lights in the shade. By the side of the soul-enchanting verses of Chaim Nachman Bialik, Saul Tchernichovsky, Da-

vid Shimonowitz, David Fichman, Asher Barasch, Shimon
Ginzburg and many others who grew up from their childhood with the Hebrew they had inherited from all by-gone
generations and whose muse was so loftily inspired by the
Hebraic culture and spiritual traditions of their people—
how feeble must have sounded the tones emitted by Elisheva's
tender lyre! Could she, the outsider, who asked to be taken
in by the Jews—this strange people so mighty in spirit, so
proud of its past and so sanguine of its future—could she,
the daughter of an alien race, hope to stand in the presence
of these mighty spirits of Israel and maintain her position
as a writer and poet? Is it not asking and assuming too much
to expect even for a moment to be worthy of the company of
these sons of the Prophets? Is it not wrong for her to push
her way among men whose gigantic dimensions would only
bring into greater relief her own dwarfish stature?

This, as I see it, is the most likely source of the great bit-
terness which gnawed at the heart of this noble-minded
woman. And yet, had Elisheva not been so super-sensitive
and so obsessed with the thought of her own inferiority—in
other words, had she not been so refined of spirit, she could
have found much comfort in the fact that her poetry had
much to recommend it for its own sake. Her muse needed
no sensational fanfares to proclaim its merits. Though Chris-
tian-born and a comparative new-comer in the realm of
Hebrew letters, Elisheva writes a Hebrew which for style and
beauty of diction may well be the envy of native-born Hebraists, and the same holds true not only of her verses but
of her essays as well. It is true that as a novelist and sketch
writer her efforts have been poor, her heroes pale and un-
convincing. This is especially exemplified in her larger work
"Simtaot" (Alleys), which is deficient as to plot and the
characters she brings upon the scene are bloodless and un-

real. Yet her essay on the Russian poet Alexander Block
(published in "Hatekufah" vols. 21-22) is a noteworthy
study in literary criticism and deserves a place among the
best essays of the sort in contemporary Hebrew letters. But
it is definitely as a poet that she excels. As I write this I am
fresh under the impact of her verses which I have just re-
read. It is lyric poetry at its best. Elisheva captivates you
by her moodiness, her sadness, her description of nature and
of the influence sun—or moonlight, lovely weather, flowers
and the chirping of birds exert upon her. She sings of love
and of beauty, of spring days and summer nights, of mystic
forest whispers and the secrets of placidly flowing streams.
Life to her is a maze of surprises and constantly revealing
wonders. And relishing her lyrical efforts one cannot, at the
same time, suppress his sense of wonder at how she managed
to perfect herself in a language not so easy to adopt—especially for adults—as is the Hebrew, and how she acquired
so rich a vocabulary with its multiplicity of shades and
nuances of expression, which would do credit to any eminent
Hebrew writer.

She was buried in Tiberias, on the shore of the Sea of
Galilee, perhaps the most picturesque spot of that beautiful
little land and a fit sepulchre for so gentle a soul. I wonder
what were Elisheva's last thoughts as she contemplated the
eternity towards which she was headed. Did she bid farewell
to the world in a spirit of bitter frustration at her apparent
failure, as she saw it? Her reward lies not in what she received but in what she gave. She came to Israel as a stranger
and, despite all her hardships and disappointments, remained an integral part of the resuscitated people and one of
its leading benefactors. Her image will always haunt me as
one of the noblest types of womanhood it was ever my good
fortune to meet.

Index